CONTENTS

Forgotten Angels

The lives of African American women who
served as nurses in the Civil War

KALINDA PAGE

JACK MCELROY

ISBN: 9798682626816

DEDICATION

To Keira

ACKNOWLEDGMENTS

Thanks to Steve Restelli for discovering and providing the world with a new photograph of Susie King Taylor, and to Marlene Rivero and Matt Buckner for keeping the memory of Ann Bradford Stokes alive and contributing an image to this book.

Thanks to Jane E. Schultz, whose scholarship helped inspire this book.

Special thanks to Sharon for her buoyant good humor and support and to Deb and Anthony, as always, for their patience and love.

INTRODUCTION

A fter the Civil War began, many women signed up to care for sick and wounded soldiers. One was Louisa May Alcott of Boston. She had just turned 30 years old in 1862 when she traveled to Washington, D.C., where the hospitals were filled with men who were ill or

Louisa May Alcott (Courtesy Library of Congress)

injured from the war. She worked as a nurse for a few weeks. But then she got sick, too, with a deadly disease called typhoid fever. Louisa almost died and had to go home to Boston. After she recovered, she published a book called *Hospital Sketches* about her time as a nurse. That launched her writing career. Within a few years, Louisa had written another book about growing up with three sisters. *Little Women* became one of the most popular American novels of all time.

Louisa May Alcott is remembered for her work as a Civil War nurse as well as for being a fine author. But there is a part of her story that many people do not know. While she was sick, another woman fought to keep her alive. Her name was Matilda Cleaver John, and she was African American. Matilda spent much of the Civil War working as a nurse, not only at the hospital where she cared for Louisa, but at three other hospitals, as well. Today, though, she is mostly forgotten. We know almost nothing about her life or about the lives of the many other Black women who worked as nurses during the Civil War. They are among our nation's unsung heroes.

1

On the Union side, more than 2,000 African American women worked in paid jobs in hospitals during the war. Many others served as unpaid volunteers. About 400 of them were officially called nurses. But that respected title usually was given only to white women who cared for the sick and wounded. Black workers more often were called cooks, laundresses, or maids. Yet many had the same duties as the white nurses, tasks that included feeding and washing patients, giving them medicine, changing their beds, and making them comfortable in any way possible.

Few records tell us who these women were, especially if they worked on the Confederate side. Thousands of enslaved women cared for the sick and wounded in the Rebel states, and not even their names were noted. We do, however, know the stories of a few Black nurses on the Union side. They were lucky enough to have learned to read and write, so they recorded their own histories. Or they

Black and white aid workers with the United States Christian Commission in Washington, D.C., in 1865 (Courtesy Library of Congress)

had other people who wrote down their stories in books or government records.

This book tells about seven of those women: Charlotte Forten Grimké, Sojourner Truth, Susie King Taylor, Rebecca Lee Crumpler, Ann Bradford Stokes, Harriet Tubman, and Sallie Daffin. The seven came from many walks of life. Charlotte grew up in a well-to-do family that had known freedom for generations. Susie and Ann were enslaved when the war began and escaped. Rebecca and Sallie were born free and were well educated. Sojourner and Harriet were born into slavery and never learned to read or write, but before the Civil War even started, they had freed themselves and earned fame.

The women had much in common, though. They were driven by strong faith. Sojourner was a preacher before she was a nurse. Sallie lived her life in the service to her church. Harriet had visions that guided her beliefs. They cared deeply for family. Susie made a desperate journey to help her son when he was dying. Charlotte inspired a niece to become an important poet. Harriet risked her life to bring her relatives together in the North. They also endured racism and discrimination. Sojourner was thrown off a segregated streetcar. Sallie saw her schoolhouse burned to the ground. Rebecca completed medical school only to be told that the "M.D." after her name stood for "mule driver," not "medical doctor."

The Civil War affected all of the women. Some nearly lost their lives. Susie survived a boating disaster. Cannon shells crashed through the hospital ship where Ann was serving. Illness threatened Charlotte's health. Others found love while in the service. Susie, Ann, and Harriet all married Civil War veterans. A few built lifelong friendships. Charlotte and Sallie lived almost next-door to each other after the war. But service as Civil War nurses was just one chapter in these women's remarkable lives. Harriet and Sojourner were fierce abolitionists before the war began, and after it ended, they added their voices to the fight for women's rights. Charlotte, Rebecca, and Sallie broke through educational barriers while growing up, and they worked to bring learning to the freed people after the war. For Ann and Susie, becoming Civil War nurses was just the start of their journeys to freedom. Afterward, they built lives that continued their march toward liberty and justice.

The women were groundbreakers in many ways. Harriet was the first Black woman to help direct a U.S. military attack. Sojourner was one of the first African Americans to win a lawsuit against a white man. Rebecca was the first Black female to become a medical doctor. Susie was the only African American woman to publish a book about serving in a Civil War regiment. Sallie united white and Black citizens in the South against racism. Ann was the first woman of any race to win a pension for her own service in the United States military.

But these seven women were not alone in their achievements. Their stories must stand for the unheralded histories of Matilda Cleaver John and thousands of other African American nurses of the Civil War whose contributions have been forgotten. They did more in their lives to shape America for the better than we will ever know.

CHARLOTTE FORTEN GRIMKE´

Charlotte Forten surely was nervous as she walked into Higginson School in Salem, Massachusetts. She was just 16 years old, more than 300 miles away from home, and entering a classroom for the first time in her life. Not only that, the private school was filled with white girls. She was African American, and the year was 1853. In many states, people of African ancestry were enslaved, and in other states, Black Americans could not attend school with white students. That, in fact, was why Charlotte was here, so far away from home. Her family refused to put her in the segregated schools in Philadelphia, Pennsylvania, where she had grown up. Instead, her father sent her to Salem, where children of all races could learn together. Charlotte was ready, though, and she knew it. She had been well educated at home -- and an extraordinary home it was. In those days of

Charlotte Forten (Courtesy New York Public Library's Digital Library)

slavery and segregation, the Fortens not only were well respected, they were wealthy, thanks to Charlotte's remarkable grandfather.

James Forten was born free in Philadelphia in 1766, ten years before the United States declared its independence from Great Britain. His own grandfather had been enslaved but had freed himself, and the Fortens had lived as free people ever since. James was very young when his father died. At the age of seven he started working to help his mother. He was a chimney sweep for a while, climbing into chimneys to clean out the soot and ash. Later he worked as a store clerk. But he still found time to go to school at Philadelphia's African School, run by a man who hated slavery and wanted to see Black children get ahead.

By the time James was a teenager, America was fighting the Revolutionary War. He signed up to fight on a warship called the Royal Louis. But the Royal Louis was captured by the British, and James was locked in a prison ship outside of New York City. Life was brutal there. Thousands of captured soldiers and sailors were crammed below decks, and every day many died. James managed to survive, though, and was released after half a year. He walked home to his mother almost 100 miles away.

Later, James sailed to England on a trading ship, and he worked in a shipyard in London for more than a year. There he heard voices speaking out against the sale of human beings. He made a promise to himself to return to the United States and join the fight against slavery. When he got back to Philadelphia, James went to work as a sailmaker. He was such a good worker that the owner of the business made him a foreman and later sold the business to him. James proved to be a clever businessman. He invented a tool that made sail-making easier, and he built a fortune worth more than $100,000. That was like having millions of dollars today.

James Forten (Courtesy Historical Society of Pennsylvania)

James Forten bought a large house, and he and his wife had eight children. But he never forgot his vow to fight slavery. He became a leader in the anti-slavery movement in Pennsylvania. Abolitionists from other parts of the United States -- including the famous journalist William Lloyd Garrison -- met in his home to discuss how to end the horror of human bondage. When James died in 1842, his funeral was one of the biggest in the history of Philadelphia. Thousands of African Americans and hundreds of white Americans marched with his coffin to the cemetery where he was buried.

James's children carried on his fight. Charlotte's father, Robert Forten, became an outspoken abolitionist, too, and her Aunt Harriet married a man named Robert Purvis, whose father had gotten rich by selling cotton. Robert Purvis used the money he inherited to help enslaved people escape to the North. Folks later called him the "Father of the Underground Railroad." Sometimes Charlotte lived with her Aunt Harriet and Uncle Robert in their beautiful country home outside Philadelphia, as well as at her father's house in the city.

But wealth did not protect the Fortens from the injustices that Black Americans faced. Charlotte and her family were not allowed to shop in many stores or eat in certain restaurants. They had to sit in segregated seats in railroad cars and were called vicious names when they went out in public. Charlotte even watched in shock as people who had escaped slavery were rounded up on the streets of Philadelphia and returned in chains to the South.

Living in Massachusetts opened new doors for Charlotte, and she soon began making her own mark on the world as a writer. She kept a journal and started writing poetry. Although she found it hard to make friends with the white girls in her class, the principal at Higginson School was caring and supportive. When Charlotte graduated in 1855, one of her poems, called "A Parting Hymn," was chosen as the class's best poem. It was put to music and sung during the graduation ceremony. That same month, another of Charlotte's poems was published in *The Liberator,* a national newspaper owned by the Fortens' friend, William Lloyd Garrison.

Encouraged by her teachers, Charlotte decided to continue her studies. She enrolled in Salem Normal School. (A normal school was what we now call a teachers'

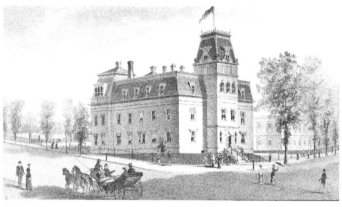

Salem Normal School (Courtesy Salem State University)

college. Salem Normal School is now named Salem State University.) She was the school's first African American student, and in 1856 she became its first Black graduate. Again, one of her poems was read during graduation. Charlotte wrote in her journal that her success at Salem Normal was "the happiest of my life … the few friends I have made are warm and true." But she could not escape the racism that was so widespread. It hurt her deeply. One day she was so upset that she wrote that Black Americans "have everything to make us hate mankind."

Still, Charlotte forged ahead. She landed a job teaching at a grammar school, becoming the first African American teacher in the Salem School District. What was really unusual was that she was a Black woman teaching white children. A local newspaper praised her work and saluted the school district for hiring her. Unfortunately, Charlotte became ill. The illness probably was tuberculosis, a disease that was widespread in those days. She had to leave her job and return to her uncle's country home to rest. Charlotte would struggle with health problems for the rest of her life. Over the next few years, she went back to Salem three times to teach. But each time her poor health forced her back to Philadelphia. She kept writing poems, though, such as *The Slave Girl's Prayer,* which pushed for an end to slavery. By then, the issue was tearing America apart.

In 1861, the Civil War began when southern states left the Union and Rebel cannons blasted Fort Sumter in the harbor of Charleston, South Carolina. A few months later, the Union Navy attacked the coast near Charleston. Thousands of enslaved people lived in this area, called the Sea Islands. When Union troops arrived, the plantation owners fled, and suddenly the African American people were free. The federal government wanted to help them adjust, so teachers were asked to go south to teach children who had never had a chance to go to school. Charlotte was the first African American to volunteer.

In 1862, she sailed south to the Sea Islands. Life was hard there. The weather was blazing in the summer and frigid in the winter. Teachers had to

Schoolhouse for freed children on the Sea Islands (Courtesy Library of Congress)

use broken furniture from deserted farmhouses. Bugs were everywhere, and diseases were a threat. Sometimes 140 children squeezed into one classroom. The students wore ragged clothes, and older children brought their baby brothers and sisters to class because their parents had to work in the fields. The children spoke with an accent that Charlotte could barely understand. But she worked hard to teach them to read and write. She also led them in songs and told stories of Black heroes such as Toussaint L'Ouverture, who led a revolution of enslaved people in the nation of Haiti.

"I never before saw children so eager to learn," Charlotte said in an article she wrote for a magazine in the North. "Coming to school is a constant delight and recreation to them. They come here as other children go to play. The older ones, during the summer, work in the fields from early morning until eleven or twelve o'clock, and then come into school, after their hard toil in the hot sun, as bright and as anxious to learn as ever."

Charlotte was lonely, though. The freedmen -- as the formerly enslaved people were called -- were friendly. But their lives were quite different from the world Charlotte had known in Philadelphia and Salem. Worse, many of the white soldiers were disrespectful to Black Americans. They treated Charlotte with scorn. There were exceptions, though. One Union officer was especially kind and polite. He was Colonel Robert Shaw, who commanded the 54th Massachusetts Infantry, a regiment led by white officers but made up of African American soldiers.

Charlotte described Shaw and the volunteers in her article: "We saw his regiment on dress-parade, and admired its remarkably fine and manly appearance," she wrote. "After taking supper with the Colonel we sat outside the tent, while some of his men entertained us with excellent singing. … How full of life and hope and lofty aspirations he was that night!" The Black soldiers were working as laborers, but Shaw wanted them to fight the Rebels. "I do hope they will give us a chance," he told Charlotte. He knew his troops would prove they were as brave as any men.

Colonel Robert Shaw (Courtesy Library of Congress)

The 54th Massachusetts got its chance on July 18, 1863. The regiment was sent to attack Fort Wagner, which guarded

An illustration of the 54th Massachusetts Infantry attacking Fort Wagner (Courtesy State Archives of North Carolina/Wikimedia Commons)

Charleston. The Black soldiers fought with great courage, charging high walls in the face of heavy cannon and rifle fire. Of the 600 men in the regiment, almost half were killed, wounded, or captured. Shaw died leading the men. The bravery of the troops showed that African Americans were gallant soldiers, and thousands more were recruited into the Union Army to help win the war.

Charlotte was heartbroken when she heard of the dead and wounded. "To-night comes news, oh, so sad, so heart sickening," she wrote. "It is too terrible, too terrible to write." In the days that followed, she went from being a teacher to being a nurse. As the wounded soldiers returned from the battlefield, she cared for them, sometimes tending to their wounds, sometimes helping them write letters, other times just sitting with them and offering comfort.

"One poor fellow here interests me greatly," she wrote. "He is very young, only nineteen, comes from Michigan. He is very badly wounded -- in both legs, and there is a ball -- in the stomach -- it is thought that it cannot be extracted. This poor fellow suffers terribly. His groans are pitiful to hear. But he utters no complaint ... Another, a Sergeant, suffers great pain, being badly wounded in the leg. But he too lies perfectly patient and uncomplaining ... He is said to be one of the best and bravest men in the regiment."

Charlotte worked in the Sea Islands until 1864, when her health again began to fail. She also got some terrible news around that time. When President Abraham Lincoln called for African Americans to join the Union Army, Charlotte's father, Robert, signed up, even though he was more than 50 years old. Soon he was promoted. But in April of that year, he caught typhoid fever and died. He was remembered as a great man and became the first Black American to be buried with full military honors. Charlotte returned to Philadelphia to heal her body and her soul.

In the years that followed, Charlotte continued to work as a teacher and to fight for civil rights. In 1872, she moved to Washington, D.C., to take a job at the city's only high school for African American youths going to college. She later went to work for the U.S. Treasury Department. In Washington, D.C., she met Reverend Francis Grimké, who had escaped enslavement during the war and gone to school to become a minister. He and Charlotte fell in love and married in 1878. On New Year's Day of 1880, their only child was born. They named her Theodora Cornelia.

Sadly, little Theodora died when she was about six months old. But later, the Grimkés did serve as guardians to a teenage niece, Angelina Weld Grimké. Angelina became a poet just like her aunt and wrote plays and stories about the wrongs suffered by African Americans. In time, she became a leader of the Black arts movement called the Harlem Renaissance.

Angelina Weld Grimké Reverend Francis Grimke´

Charlotte, too, continued to write poems, essays, and letters pointing to the injustices Black Americans faced. She also helped start the National Association of Colored Women, which fought for justice for women and African Americans. Despite her health problems, she lived to be 76. She died on July 23, 1914, in Washington. Her husband lived for another 22 years, never remarrying. Francis helped start the National Association for the Advancement of Colored People, which became America's leading civil rights organization. He and Charlotte are buried just outside Washington, and their home today is on the National Register of Historic Places.

Charlotte's journal was published 38 years after her death. In it, she described how she felt growing up in the days of slavery and being part of the fight for liberation. Something she wrote while working on the Sea Islands also made a bit of history. After a night of listening to the sounds of suffering among the freed people, she had gone to church the following day. Afterward she wrote: "I came home with the blues. Threw myself on the bed and for the first time since I have been here, felt very lonesome and pitied myself. But I have reasoned myself into a more sensible mood and feel better now." This may be the first time any American writer referred to having "the blues." Today Americans often use that term when they want to describe a feeling of sadness, or if they are talking about the style of music that Black Americans invented to celebrate staying strong in the face of hardship.

Charlotte Forten Grimke´ (Courtesy Wikimedia Commons)

SOJOURNER TRUTH

Sojourner Truth (Courtesy New York Public Library Digital Collections)

People know the story of Rosa Parks, the civil rights worker who refused to give up her seat on a bus to a white passenger. Her heroic stand in 1955 started the freedom movement that brought an end to segregation laws in the United States. But do they remember that 90 years earlier another civil rights hero refused to give up her seat on a streetcar as she fought to integrate our nation's capital? She was Sojourner Truth, who was working as a nurse in Washington, D.C., during the Civil War. Sojourner did much more than that, though. Over her long life, she was a preacher, an author, and a leader in the struggles for African American and women's rights. She was a mother, too, who fought to protect her children and build a better life for them. She did all this even though she started her life in slavery and never had a chance to learn to read or write.

Sojourner was born in 1797, just 10 years after the U.S. Constitution was written. Her parents were enslaved on a farm in a part of New York settled by the Dutch, and that was the language they spoke there. Her father,

James, was tall and straight. He went by the last name of Bomefree, which was taken from the Dutch word for "tree," or "boom." Her mother, Betsey, was known as "Mau-Mau Bet," from the Dutch word for "Mama." Sojourner was named Isabella when she was born, and she was called Bell for many years. James and Betsey had at least 10 children. Bell was the second youngest, and she never knew many of her older brothers and sisters. They had been sold away by the time she was just a baby.

Statue of young Sojourner Truth in Ulster County, New York (Courtesy Vagirl38/CC By-SA)

When she was nine, Bell was sold, too. Her new owner spoke English and got angry when Bell could not understand him. One day, he tied her hands and whipped her with sticks until her back was bloody. She carried the scars from that beating for the rest of her life. That owner sold Bell again, and she ended up on a farm owned by John and Sally Dumont. Life was better there, though still very hard. She worked in the fields, cleaned the house, weaved cloth, cooked, and took care of babies. She was such a hard worker that one of the white girls who also worked there became jealous. While Bell was out milking the cows, the girl threw ashes in the potatoes Bell had been cooking. The girl wanted to get Bell into trouble by making the potatoes gray. But the Dumonts' 10-year-old daughter saw what happened and told her mother. It was the white girl who ended up being punished instead of Bell.

Bell tried to keep in touch with her parents. She asked permission to visit them and sometimes was allowed to go to their nearby farm. Enslavement wore her parents down. Her father went blind and lost his strength. He depended on Mau-Mau for everything. Then one day she collapsed and died. The last time Bell tried to see her father, she walked 12 miles only to find out that he was in a new place 20 miles away. When James grew too weak to work at all, he was set free. But Bell never saw him again.

When she was about 18, Bell fell in love with a man named Robert who was enslaved on another farm. The farm owner tried to keep the two apart, but Robert found ways to sneak off and visit Bell. One day he was caught. The farmer beat him, tied him up, and dragged him away. Still, the couple had a daughter together. Bell named her Diana. Later, Dumont forced Bell to marry an older man named Thomas. They had three children who survived: Elizabeth, Peter, and Sophia. When Bell worked in the fields, she took her babies with her. She would put them in a basket hanging from a tree. There they could swing and be safe from snakes.

New York began changing its laws to end slavery. One new law said that anyone born after 1799 would be set free when they became adults. Bell had been born too soon to be helped by that. But another law said that other people would be freed on July 4, 1827. Dumont made a deal with Bell. If she worked hard, she would have her freedom a year early, in 1826. She did work hard, even though she hurt her hand. When the time for freedom came, though, Dumont broke his promise. He claimed that because Bell was injured, she had not done enough work and she would have to remain enslaved for another year. This made Bell furious. She stayed on the Dumont farm long enough to spin 100 pounds of wool. She figured that would make up for any work she had not done. Then she left, taking her baby daughter, Sophia, with her. "I did not run off," Bell declared, "I walked off, believing that to be all right."

But she had no idea where to go. She prayed for help and ended up at the home of Isaac and Maria Van Wagenen. They proved to be kind people who hated slavery. When Dumont tracked Bell down and tried to force her to come back to his farm, the Van Wagenens gave him $20 to let her stay. Bell's troubles with Dumont were not over, though. She had left her other children behind, and one day she heard some awful news. Under New York law, enslaved people could not be sold out of the state. But Dumont had sold Bell's son Peter, who was just five years old, and the new owner had taken the boy to Alabama, far away in the South. Bell tried everything to get Peter back. Finally, some members of the Quaker church helped her go to court and file a lawsuit. She won. Bell was one of the first African Americans to sue a white man and win. After months away, Peter was returned to his mother. But he was scarred and afraid, and never quite the same.

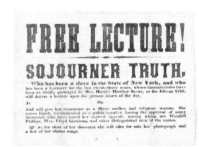

Lecture poster (Courtesy Berenice Bryant Lowe Papers, Bentley Library, University of Michigan)

After Peter's return, Bell's life changed again. God, she believed, had visited her. She began to attend a local church, then moved to New York City and joined a religious group. She worked as a housekeeper for the group's leader, and her English improved. She could not read, but she listened and learned the lessons of the Bible. Soon she was doing some preaching herself. Bell had grown very tall -- almost six feet -- and she was a forceful speaker. As the years went by, more and more people heard about her and came to listen to what she had to say.

Bell believed that New York City was no place for her daughters. They remained on farms, and she kept in touch with them there. Peter stayed with her, though. As he grew into a teenager, he started to get into trouble, and Bell worried about him. But when he was 18, some of her friends helped him get a job on a whaling ship, and he set sail. As he traveled the world for the next couple of years, he wrote to his mother. Then the letters stopped, and Bell never heard from him again. She grieved for many years.

In 1843, Bell heard God's voice again. He told her to leave New York City and start a new life. "The Spirit calls me, and I must go," she told her friends. That new life included a new name: Sojourner Truth. The name meant she would journey across the land and speak the truth about what she saw. Sojourner's travels took her to a farm in Massachusetts where more than 200 people lived and worked together. The group believed in rights for women and freedom for African Americans.

SOJOURNER TRUTH.

Drawing of Sojourner Truth printed with her *Narrative* (Courtesy Carl A. Kroch Library, Cornell University)

There she met some of the country's leading abolitionists, including Frederick Douglass. Like Sojourner, he had fled enslavement and become a well-known speaker. Now he was writing a book about his life. When it was published, people were amazed by his story and bought thousands of copies. Douglass encouraged Sojourner to talk about what she had endured in slavery, and she became an outspoken abolitionist, too. She decided that the story of her life would make an interesting book, as well. Because she could not read or write, she dictated the book to a friend. The *Narrative of Sojourner Truth* was published in 1850. She sold it for 25 cents a copy at her speeches, and she made enough money to buy a house. Her fame grew, and she was invited to speak across the country.

Sojourner's most famous speech came a few years later at the Ohio Women's Rights Convention. A man in the crowd yelled that women were weak and needed to be helped by men. "That man over there says that women need to be helped into carriages, and lifted over ditches," Sojourner answered. "Nobody ever helps me into carriages, or over mud puddles ... and ain't I a woman? ... I have plowed, and planted, and gathered into barns ... I could work as much and eat as much as a man (when I could get it), and bear the lash as well -- and ain't I a woman?" Many newspapers wrote about the "Ain't I a Woman" speech. Sojourner became known as a champion for women as well as for African Americans. But because she was so tall and forceful, some people claimed she was not really a woman. She was not ashamed to prove them wrong. At one speech, when someone shouted that she was really a man, she angrily opened the front of her dress to show her "mother's breasts." Another time, when people asked if slavery really was so bad, she turned around, lowered her dress, and showed the scars on her back where she had been beaten.

Sojourner Truth with a photograph of grandson James Caldwell in her lap (Courtesy Library of Congress)

In 1857, Sojourner moved to Battle Creek, Michigan. All three of her daughters -- Diana, Elizabeth and Sophia -- came to live with her, along with their husbands and other family members. One special family member was Sojourner's grandson James Caldwell. He often traveled with his grandmother and helped her as she grew older. In 1861, the Civil War began.

When the Union Army allowed African Americans to join, James was one of the first to sign up. "Now is our time, Grandmother, to prove that we are men," he told her. He joined the 54th Massachusetts Infantry, one of the nation's first military units made up of Black Americans.

Sojourner was proud. "My grandson has enlisted," she told everyone. But tragedy struck. James was in the regiment's very first battle, and he was wounded and captured. His family had no idea what had happened to him. They only knew that the Confederates hated African American soldiers and abused them as prisoners. James survived, but he suffered greatly and was weak and disturbed after he was released.

In those days, one of the most famous writers was Harriet Beecher Stowe. Her book, *Uncle Tom's Cabin,* revealed the horrors of slavery and stirred up feelings across the country before the war. When President Abraham Lincoln met her, he joked that she was "the little woman who wrote the book that started this great war." The author had met Sojourner and her grandson when James was just a young boy. After Lincoln announced the Emancipation Proclamation declaring the end of slavery in the South, Harriet Beecher Stowe wrote an article about Sojourner that was published in a national magazine. It added to her fame.

Painting of President Lincoln showing Sojourner Truth a Bible from freed people in Maryland (Courtesy Library of Congress)

As the war continued, Sojourner worked to assist the people who were escaping. She gathered donations, packed boxes, and prepared meals for them. Soon thousands of freed people were pouring into Washington, D.C., crowding the city. The national government hired Sojourner to help. She moved to the capital, and while she was there, she met with President Lincoln. They talked about ending slavery, and he showed her a Bible that had been given to him by Black Americans in Maryland. Sojourner said afterward, "I never was treated by anyone with more kindness and cordiality than was shown to me by that great and good man."

A hospital was set up in Washington to care for the freed people, and Sojourner became a nurse there. Old homeless men and women lived their last days at the Freedmen's Hospital, suffering from aches, pains, and tremors. Mothers and small children were sick with typhoid fever and smallpox. Soldiers were wounded and ill. The nurses tried to keep the hospital clean, but that was hard. Many patients shared just one washroom. Sojourner was nearly 70 years old by then. The work tired her, and cold drafts made her legs hurt.

A horse-drawn streetcar in Washington, D.C. (Courtesy General Photograph Collection, Historical Society of Washington, D.C.)

Besides working in the hospital, she traveled around the city, visiting an orphanage, collecting supplies, and caring for people who were too weak to leave their homes. Streetcars were the way to get around. These horse-drawn rail cars were the buses of the 1800s. At first, Black Americans were not allowed to ride with white people. Before the end of the war, though, the government changed the law so that the races could ride together. But many streetcar conductors still tried to keep African Americans off. Sojourner knew the law and insisted on her rights.

One day, when she was getting on a streetcar, the driver quickly pulled away. Sojourner hung on and was dragged along until she was able to climb onto the car. She complained, and the man was fired. Another time when she was waiting, a driver drove past, pretending he did not see her. When the next streetcar came along, Sojourner waved her hand and shouted: "I want to ride. I want to ride! I WANT TO RIDE!" She was so loud she stopped all the traffic in the street. After she climbed aboard, the conductor told her to get off, but she refused.

A few weeks later, she was with a white friend bringing supplies to the

Freedmen's Hospital. The two women got on a streetcar together, but the conductor told Sojourner to get off. Again, she refused. He grabbed her arm and threw her to the ground, hurting her shoulder. When the doctors at the hospital heard what happened, they had the streetcar conductor arrested. Because of Sojourner's persistence and courage, Black and white people soon were riding streetcars together. The cars, she said, "looked like pepper and salt."

After the war, Congress began debating whether African American men should be allowed to vote. The issue divided people who had joined together in the fight against slavery. At that time, no women at all could vote. Women's rights leaders, such as Susan B. Anthony, thought it was more important for white women to get the vote than for Black men. Frederick Douglass believed it was "a matter of life and death" for African American men to vote while women could wait. Sojourner, now in her 70s, was active in the debate, making speeches arguing for the rights of African American women. In 1870, the 15th Amendment passed, giving Black men the right to vote. But women of all races were not allowed to vote until 50 years later, when the 19th Amendment to the Constitution became law.

Sojourner Truth monument in Michigan (Courtesy battlecreekcvb/CC By 2.0)

In her final years, Sojourner asked the government to give land west of the Mississippi River to people who had been enslaved. Her petition failed, but freed people left the South and moved west anyway. By 1880, more than 40,000 African Americans had moved to Kansas. While in her 80s, Sojourner traveled through Kansas to help the settlers. But the work took a toll on her health. She spent her last years at her home in Michigan, cared for by daughters Diana and Elizabeth. Newspaper reporters often visited her there. They wanted to interview the woman who had risen from slavery to become one of the most famous and respected people in America.

Sojourner Truth died on November 26, 1883, at the age of 86. Statues of her now stand in many cities, and she was the first African American woman to have a bust displayed in the U.S. Capitol. Her face has been on postage stamps, and she is a member of the National Women's Hall of Fame. When the United States landed a spacecraft on Mars, the rover that explored the planet was named Sojourner in honor of this woman who made it her mission in life to "travel up and down the land" in the cause of freedom.

SUSIE KING TAYLOR

When she was 13, Susie Baker's life changed forever. As the dogwood trees were blooming in Georgia, cannons started thundering in the distance. It was April 1862. Union forces were attacking Fort Pulaski, which guarded the Rebel city of Savannah. Susie could hear the guns roar. "They jarred the earth for miles," she remembered. The noise was frightful, but hopeful, too. She and her family were enslaved on a nearby plantation, and the guns were a call to freedom. Soon the Confederates in the fort surrendered and Union troops moved in. Two days later, Susie fled the plantation with her uncle and his family. The group made its way to the Union lines. "To my unbounded joy," Susie recalled, "I saw the 'Yankee.'" She knew she was free. What she did not know was that soon she would join with African American soldiers fighting to bring freedom to others and be on her way to a life of leadership and honor.

Susie King Taylor (Courtesy Library of Congress)

The Baker family had been held in bondage for generations. Susie's elders shared stories about her great-great-grandmother, who was half Native American and from Virginia. She lived to be 120 years old, they said. Susie's

21

great-grandmother lived in Savannah. She had 24 children, 23 of them girls. One of those girls was Susie's grandmother, Dolly. Dolly had two children, James and Hagar Ann. James died when he was 12. But Hagar Ann grew up to marry Raymond Baker, and their first child was the girl they named Susan Ann. Everyone called her Susie.

Slavery in the South was cruel. But Mr. and Mrs. Grest, who owned the farm where Susie lived, showed her some kindness. When she was seven, they allowed her to move to Savannah, where Grandmother Dolly lived like a free woman. Susie always remembered that special day, riding to the city in a wagon driven by a man with a beard that reached nearly to his knees. Dolly was a hard worker who made a decent living by trading tobacco, flour, and sugar from the city for chicken and eggs from the countryside. She had greater hopes for her granddaughter's future.

Enslaved people on Georgia plantation before Civil War (Courtesy Wikimedia Commons)

Susie was a bright girl, and Dolly sent her to school even though that was against the law. Before the Civil War, the Georgia government let only white children learn to read and write. Teachers were whipped for teaching African Americans. Susie and her fellow students sneaked to a secret classroom with their books wrapped in paper to hide them. She quickly learned her ABCs and advanced to another school where the teacher taught Susie "all she knew." Susie wanted to know more, though. She asked a white playmate to teach her, and the girl agreed, so long as her father did not find out. Then a boy in high school gave Susie more lessons. But by then, the Civil War had started, and the young man marched off with the Rebel army.

Savannah was tense in those days. Black Americans needed passes written by white people to move around the city. Anyone caught without a pass could be thrown in jail. Susie was so good at writing by then that she forged passes for friends and signed Mr. Grest's name. The white planters were afraid that African Americans would run away as the Yankees grew closer. They spread rumors that the Northerners would treat runaways like horses and make them pull carts. Grandmother Dolly scoffed at the idea. "'Certainly not,'" she said. "The Yankee was going to set all the slaves free."

People prayed for freedom to come. One night, when Dolly went to a church meeting, everyone sang: "Yes, we all shall be free / Yes, we all shall be free / Yes, we all shall be free / When the Lord shall appear." Police heard the song and raided the church, putting the worshippers in jail. Luckily, Dolly was not kept locked up. But Susie was sent back to the Grest plantation. It was from there that she made her escape a few days later.

A family on the Sea Islands near Savannah during war (Courtesy Library of Congress)

Susie and her family found protection on the Sea Islands along the Georgia coast. Rich farmland covered these islands, where fine cotton was grown. Many African Americans had been enslaved there. But when the Union forces arrived, the plantation owners fled, leaving the workers behind. Susie and her relatives joined thousands of other refugees seeking freedom on the islands.

One day, a group of about 30 were sailing from one island to the next. The boat captain asked Susie if she could read and write. Yes, she said. "He handed me a book and a pencil and told me to write my name and where I was from. I did this," Susie remembered. The captain was impressed. He told a senior officer, and three days later, Susie was asked to set up a school on the island. Two boxes of books soon arrived. Within a few weeks, Susie was teaching 40 of the escaped children each day. At night, adults came, and she taught them to read and write, as well.

At first, the Union government did not know what to do with all the people who were escaping enslavement. The general in charge of the Sea Islands, David Hunter, hated slavery. He wanted the runaways to live in freedom, and he wanted African American men to become soldiers and fight the Confederates. He formed a regiment called the First South Carolina Volunteers. Young men, tasting liberty for the first time, were eager to join. Several of Susie's uncles and cousins enlisted in the regiment. So did Edward King, a special friend who, like Susie, could read and write. Colonel Thomas Higginson, a white officer and abolitionist, was put in command of the volunteers. Edward was named a sergeant, the highest rank held by Black troops. The soldiers were the first African Americans to join the Union Army. Soon they were battling any Rebels left on the Sea Islands. Susie joined the regiment, too. Her official job laundress. But as men got sick or were wounded, she found herself serving more and more as a nurse. She had just turned 14.

On New Year's Day, 1863, the Emancipation Proclamation took effect. President Abraham Lincoln declared that all people held in slavery in the Rebel states were free. Steamboats brought the freed people of the Sea Islands together for a big celebration. "It was a glorious day for us all," remembered Susie. Ten oxen were roasted. The

Illustration of Emancipation Day celebration on the Sea Islands (Courtesy Wikimedia Commons)

barbecue was a "fine feast." Speeches were made, and a band played. Soldiers "sang or shouted 'Hurrah!' all through the camp," Susie recalled. The high point came when a famous preacher from New York presented a flag to the African American regiment. Just as Colonel Higginson accepted the gift, a freed woman in the crowd began singing "America" and everyone joined in: "My country 'tis of thee / Sweet land of liberty / Of thee I sing." For Susie, that New Year's Day was a time of personal celebration, too. She and Sergeant King had fallen in love, and around that time, they got married.

After the new year, the fighting grew fierce for the South Carolina Volunteers. Within a few weeks they joined an attack on Jacksonville, Florida. Rebel soldiers blackened their faces so that the Union troops would think they, too, were African Americans. "Our boys halted a second, saying, 'They are black men! Let them come to us," remembered Susie. Then, "the firing was opened and several of our men were wounded and killed."

A spy discovered where Colonel Higginson had set up his headquarters, and that night the Confederates aimed their cannons there. Susie was camped just behind the colonel. "I expected every moment to be killed by a shell," she said. She hurried away, out of range of the guns.

Months later, the regiment attacked Fort Gregg outside of Charleston, South Carolina. Susie waited in camp with a friend. "It was lonesome and sad, now that the boys were gone, some never to return," she said. The two women shared a tent that night, but fleas kept them awake. Before dawn, they heard the guns pounding. Susie rushed to the boat landing to wait for the wounded to arrive. The first was Samuel Anderson, one of Sergeant King's comrades. He was badly hurt. Others soon arrived with horrible wounds. Susie did all she could to help. Many of the men were hungry, but there

A painting of an African American regiment fighting in Florida (Courtesy Wikimedia Commons)

was little to eat. She found some milk and turtle eggs and mixed them together. "I had doubts," she said. "Cooking with turtle eggs was something new to me, but the result was a very delicious custard."

During the war, illness was a bigger problem than wounds. Many soldiers came down with smallpox, a disease that killed a third of the African Americans who caught it. Susie was not too afraid of being infected because she had been vaccinated. Still, she drank sassafras tea "constantly," she said, to prevent the disease. One man was terribly ill. Only the doctor and camp steward could see him. "But I went to see this man every day and nursed him," Susie recalled.

Around this time, Clara Barton, the famous Civil War nurse, arrived on the Sea Islands. She was shocked to see the "thousands of old, sick, lame, worn out and helpless men, women and children." The smallpox, she later wrote, was like the "terrors of the plague." She gathered medicine, blankets, food, and clothing for the freed people. Susie met her at a hospital for African American soldiers. "Miss Barton was always very cordial toward me," Susie wrote later, "and I honored her for her devotion and care of those men." The work exhausted Clara Barton, though. She left

Clara Barton (Library of Congress)

the Sea Islands and spent time recovering in a Washington, D.C., hospital.

When the freed people asked how they could thank her for her kindness, she told them to send her seashells from the area's beautiful beaches.

Susie served more than four years on the Sea Islands. She taught soldiers how to read and write. She cooked and did laundry. She also cleaned guns. She would fire them to make sure the cartridges were dry, and she learned to shoot straight and hit a target. "I was also able to take a gun all apart, and put it together again," she said.

One Christmas time, she had an adventure that almost took her life. She was sailing from one island to another with other soldiers' wives. One of the women had a two-year-old child with her. By the time they sailed, it was almost dark, and during the passage, the boat capsized. Susie slipped beneath the surface twice before she could grab the collapsed sail and hold on. The mother clutched part of the boat with one hand and her child with the other. "We drifted and shouted as loud as we could," Susie remembered. But in the dark, passing boats did not see them. Around midnight, just as the castaways were giving up hope, a woman on a nearby island heard their cries and alerted her son. Two boats rushed out to help and pulled the survivors from the water. Sadly, the toddler had died. Susie had swallowed a lot of water. She was swollen and sick and had a bad cough for a long time.

Charleston ruins after war (Mathew Brady photo courtesy U.S. National Archives)

Toward the end of the war, Susie's regiment entered Charleston, where the Civil War had begun. Rebels fleeing the city set it afire. For three or four days, the Union soldiers battled the blaze, sometimes trying to save the homes of the white people who had enslaved them. "These brave men risked life and limb," Susie remembered, even as the Southerners sneered at them. After the war finally ended, Susie and the soldiers stayed in Charleston until early 1866, when the Army released them from service. She never received a single dollar for her work. "I was glad, however, to be allowed to go with the regiment to care for the sick and afflicted comrades," she said.

In the months that followed, Susie and her husband returned to Savannah, where Edward led a crew of workers unloading ships. Susie started her own school, teaching Black children to read and write for $1 a month. Soon she was expecting a baby. It must have been a joyous time for the couple, but it did not last. Edward was killed in an accident at the pier. Then Susie had to close her school because a free school opened nearby, and her students started going there. She was forced to work as a servant, leaving her little boy with her mother while she cooked and cleaned for white families. After a few years, one of those families took Susie north to New England for the summer. She liked what she saw there. When the chance came, she moved to Boston, Massachusetts, for good. There she fell in love again and married Russell Taylor in 1879. She was 31 years old and ready to start a new life as Susie King Taylor.

Susie King Taylor's schoolhouse in Savannah (Courtesy Documenting the American South, University of North Carolina at Chapel Hill)

In the years after the Civil War, men who fought for the Union formed a group called the Grand Army of the Republic. They met in cities and towns across the country, planning ways to help veterans of the war. Women wanted to get involved, too. They started their own organization called the Women's Relief Corps. In Boston, Susie was a founding member of one of the Relief Corps groups. Over time, she was elected to all its leadership positions, including president. The Relief Corps held events to raise money for former soldiers. One year, Boston's groups organized a fair, and Susie made a red, white, and blue "Old Glory" quilt to be sold there. The quilt was so beautiful, it was given to the president of the fair. For a while, Susie and Russell ran a boarding house. They were respected members of the community. Life was good for them in New England. But in 1898, Susie was reminded of how difficult life was for Black Americans in the South, even though slavery had ended more than 30 years earlier.

That year, Susie got a message from her son, who had become an actor in a traveling theater company. He was ill in Shreveport, Louisiana. She traveled to help him and witnessed the racism that ruled the former Confederacy. When her train entered the South, she had to move into an uncomfortable, segregated car. "I have ridden in many coaches, but I was never in such as these," she said. "I wanted to return home again, but when I thought of my sick boy I said, 'Well, others ride in these cars and I must do likewise.'" In Shreveport, she found her son in bad shape. She wanted to take him home. But she was not allowed to buy a ticket for a sleeper car, and he was too sick to travel sitting up. "I was forced to let him remain where he was," Susie said. "It seemed very hard, when his father fought to protect the Union and our flag, and yet his boy was denied, under this same flag, a berth to carry him home to die."

Susie's son did die and was buried in Shreveport. While she was there, she learned that a white man had shot and killed a Black man for supposedly being "saucy" yet was not punished for the crime. The horror continued as she made her sad trip home. In Mississippi, she saw an African American lynched. Still, Susie maintained her basic optimism. "We hope for better conditions in the future," she wrote after she returned, "and feel sure they will come in time."

A recently discovered photo believed to be of Susie King Taylor (Courtesy Steve Restelli)

Susie suffered another loss after she returned from the South. Her husband Russell died in 1901. For the second time in her life, she was a widow. Yet, her spirit was unbroken. For years, people had urged her to write a book about her incredible life, and in 1902, she did. She called it *Reminiscences of My Life in Camp*. She wrote the book to "show how much service and good we can do to each other, and what sacrifices we can make for our liberty and rights."

Today, *Reminiscences* is the only published memoir by an African American woman who served in a military unit during the Civil War. Colonel Higginson, who led the 1st South Carolina Volunteers, wrote the introduction. He praised Susie as an "exceptional" woman and recommended her book to people who "love the plain record of simple lives, led in stormy times."

Susie was living and working in a hospital in Boston not long before she died in 1912 at the age of 64. Her name is preserved by the Susie King Taylor Community School in Savannah, a public school for students from kindergarten to eighth grade. In 2018, she was inducted into the Georgia Women of Achievement, honoring her contribution to that state's history.

REBECCA LEE CRUMPLER

Joyous African American men, women, and children rushed into the streets to cheer when Union soldiers marched into Richmond, Virginia, at the end of the Civil War. President Abraham Lincoln arrived in the fallen Confederate capital the following day. "You are free -- free as air," he told the people crowding around him. "You can cast off the name of slave and trample upon it. It will come to you no more." But a year later, Lincoln was dead and the freed people in Richmond were struggling. The government's Freedmen's Bureau had closed a large refugee camp and stopped providing food. Folks were homeless and hungry. Then cholera struck. The disease killed so many of the freed people that they had

A medallion honors the memory of Dr. Rebecca Lee, though the image may not be of her actual face. No photo of her is known to exist. (Courtesy Drexel University Archives and Special Collections)

to be buried in mass graves. It was then, in 1866, that Rebecca Lee Crumpler arrived in Richmond. She was there to help the sick, and she was well prepared to do it. Rebecca had spent years as a professional nurse. But she was more than a nurse now. Rebecca Lee Crumpler, M.D., had just become a doctor -- the first African American woman doctor in history.

Rebecca was born in Cristiana, Delaware, in 1831. Her parents were named Absolum Davis and Matilda Webber, though not much more is known about them. Delaware was one of America's border states. It was close to the northern states that ended slavery before the Civil War. Yet, like the states to the south, it still allowed people to be enslaved. By the time of

Rebecca's birth, though, most Black Americans in Delaware were free. It is likely, her parents had not been enslaved, and she definitely was born into freedom. But in those difficult years before the war, Delaware passed harsh laws discriminating against African Americans. They could not vote or speak in court against white people. They could not carry guns, though they had to carry identity papers signed by white officials. There were few schools for their children. Sometimes Black Americans even were arrested, or grabbed by gangs, and forced into slavery. So it was not surprising that, as a child, Rebecca left Delaware and went to live with her aunt in Pennsylvania, just a couple of days' ride by wagon to the north.

Rebecca's aunt was known as a healer in her community. Her "usefulness with the sick was continually sought," Rebecca remembered. In those days, some African American women were known to be especially wise in the ways of traditional medicine. They used herbs, spices, roots, and barks to treat illness and injury. Sap from pine trees was turned into vapor rub. Bits of plants were mixed into teas or put in small bags to hang around the necks of sick people so they could breathe in soothing smells. These women also helped deliver babies and coached new mothers on how to care for their children. As Rebecca grew up, she learned the healing arts from her aunt and decided that she, too, wanted to do everything she could to "relieve the sufferings of others."

Philadelphia, Pennsylvania, was an exciting and sometimes frightening city for a young Black girl. The year before Rebecca was born, the first national meeting of African American leaders was held there. For the next several years, Philadelphia was home to conventions where people discussed ways to end slavery and fight laws that

An illustration of the burning of Pennsylvania Hall in 1838 (Courtesy Wikimedia Commons)

harmed Black Americans. Some of the nation's most famous abolitionists came, men like Frederick Douglass and William Lloyd Garrison. When Rebecca was seven, the abolitionists built an impressive meeting place called Pennsylvania Hall. But racial tensions were high. Just four days after the building opened, a mob of white people burned it down. Its charred remains stood for many years, and Rebecca probably saw the ruins often.

More violence shook the city when she was 11. White immigrants reacted to an African American parade by rioting for three days. Many Black Americans fled the city. These events worried Rebecca and her aunt. When she became an adult, Rebecca left the city, too, and found new opportunities further north.

By the time she was 21, Rebecca was living near Boston, Massachusetts. She had followed in her aunt's footsteps and was working as a nurse. She also had met a man named Wyatt Lee, who had been enslaved in Virginia before making his way north. They fell in love, and in April 1852, they were married. Rebecca believed she was just about the right age to wed. She later shared advice for girls who were looking ahead to marriage. "It is best for a young woman to accept a suitor who is … a few years her senior, if not of an equal age," she said. "The age of a young woman should be about 19 or 20."

For the next eight years, Rebecca worked as a nurse for several doctors. She yearned to do more, though. Nurses did not need any special training in those days. The first nursing school did not open until several years after the Civil War. But Rebecca wanted formal education in her field. So she applied to medical school. This was a bold step. At the time, there were more than 50,000 doctors in the United States. Yet only 300 of them were women, and none of those were African American.

Rebecca was in luck, though. Not far from her home, a unique school had opened 10 years earlier. The New England Female Medical College was the first medical school for women in the world. When the college opened, some men complained that women were not fit to be doctors. They were not strong enough and could not handle the job because of their "sensitive and delicate nature." Women proved them wrong as dozens graduated from the school. The new role was so unusual, though, that they were given a different title. They were called "doctresses."

New England Female Medical College (Courtesy Boston University Libraries Open BU)

The male doctors who had employed Rebecca supported her application to medical school, and she was accepted. She became the first and only Black American to attend the college. Her studies included 17 weeks in the classroom followed by at least two years of training with a doctor. In addition to the usual subjects, the Female Medical College taught students the best way to deliver babies and to provide women's health care, lessons that were rare in medical schools at that time. Despite Rebecca's experience as a nurse, the work was challenging. She faced difficult exams and had to overcome personal tragedy, as well. While she was going to school, her husband, Wyatt, grew ill and died.

Rebecca received her "doctress" degree on March 1, 1864. She may not have even realized she was the first African American woman to achieve that success. She started working as a physician in Boston. About this time, she also fell in love again. Arthur Crumpler was born into slavery in Virginia in 1824 and had learned to be a blacksmith on the plantation where he lived. When the Civil War started in 1861, Arthur fled. He escaped to Fort Monroe, a Union base that the freed people called Freedom's Fortress. There Arthur used his blacksmithing skills to help the Union Army by making horseshoes. After about a year, he headed north to Boston where he met Nathaniel Allen, an abolitionist and teacher.

Allen ran a school that was way ahead of its time. The Allen School let girls and boys attend together. It had a kindergarten, one of the first in the country. It also had gym classes, which were unusual. Both white and African American students were welcome. Allen let Arthur sleep in the barn and do chores around the school. Rebecca probably met him there. Their relationship blossomed. Rebecca traveled to Canada to gain a "larger scope" of understanding about health care, and Arthur must have gone with her. In May 1865, the two were married in Saint John, Canada, up the coast from Boston.

Just a month earlier, the Civil War had ended. From the start of the conflict, the Union Army had tried to capture Richmond, the Confederate capital. After northern troops finally succeeded in April 1865, the war was over within a week. African Americans left plantations across Virginia and poured into the city. The Freedmen's Bureau tried to help them. But by the end of the year, the aid was drying up.

That winter, wood was scarce. The refugees burned whatever they could to stay warm. One old woman was found in a dark cabin dressed in rags. She had eaten only a few cabbage leaves in two days. In another dwelling, a mother and five children shared a small fire and just one blanket. The child in the woman's arms was dying. Southerners in the city resented the people who, not long ago, had been enslaved. Gangs of white youths attacked the main refugee camp in the spring. Riots broke out, and the government closed the camp, leaving many people without shelter. By the time summer ended, the Freedmen's Bureau had stopped most of its food rations. White city leaders began harassing the freed people, passing a law that locked up the homeless in chain gangs. When cholera reached Richmond that fall, Black Americans were so terrified that some believed the disease was caused by white people trying to poison them.

"My mind centered upon Richmond," Rebecca recalled when she thought back to that time. She knew she could help the poor and needy in the city as well as learn more there about the diseases affecting women and children. She moved to Richmond and joined the Freedmen's Bureau. Over the next few years, Rebecca worked with other African American doctors -- all of them men -- to care for more than 30,000 freed people in the city. She faced both racism and sexism as she worked. Some druggists would not fill her prescriptions. Other doctors snubbed her. People even joked that the "M.D." after her name stood for "mule driver" instead of "medical doctor." Rebecca never gave up. Her faith in God supported her. Richmond, she later wrote, was "a proper field for real missionary work."

Freed people in Richmond just after the Civil War (Courtesy Library of Congress)

Rebecca returned to Boston in 1869 and began practicing medicine "with renewed vigor." She took sick children into her house, whether or not their families could pay for treatment. Arthur worked as a porter, taking care of stores. Around Christmas time the following year, they had a baby girl who they named Lizzie.

Education was still an important part of Rebecca's life. She went back to her home state of Delaware twice to do some teaching. She also decided to go back to school herself to improve her math skills. She attended the integrated Allen School, where Arthur had lived and worked when he first

arrived in Boston. Arthur had never learned how to read or write, and Rebecca encouraged him to go to school, as well. But when he tried, problems with his eyesight held him back. Rebecca reassured him and said she would read to

Illustration of mourners led by Frederick Douglass paying their respects to Charles Sumner (Courtesy Library of Congress)

him. She likely read the Bible. The Crumplers were active in their Baptist church, where Arthur was a church trustee. Rebecca became one of the most respected women in the community. When Charles Sumner, a famous Massachusetts senator and abolitionist, died, she spoke at a memorial service and read a poem she had written for him.

In 1880, Rebecca stopped practicing medicine and turned her attention to a new challenge, writing a book. She called it *A Book of Medical Discourses,* and she filled it with "common sense" advice. The book included tips on feeding, washing, and dressing babies. It told girls what to do when their monthly periods began. It guided young women on choosing good husbands and having happy marriages. Rebecca warned parents to watch their children's diets: "Children should not be asked if they like such and such to eat." She even included a recipe for mixing herbs, roots, bark, and sugar to make a syrup to treat coughs and colds. Perhaps the cure was one her aunt had taught her as a girl back in Pennsylvania. The book drew on

Rebecca's experience in the Civil War, as well. A long section discussed treating cholera in infants. She dedicated the book to mothers and nurses. When it was published in 1883, it was one of the first medical texts written by an African American.

Rebecca died in Boston in 1894. She was 64 years old. After she died, her husband tried again to fulfill a dream they both had shared. Arthur went back to school, and this time he did learn to read and write. A Boston newspaper heard of his accomplishment and published an article about him with the headline: "Boston's Oldest Pupil." He told the reporter that, after Rebecca died, "I found that I should have to depend upon myself if I wanted to learn anything. I could not read the newspapers during the last war, but if we have a war now, I shall be able to read all about it myself."

Drawing of Arthur Crumpler from "Boston's Oldest Pupil" article (Courtesy The Boston Globe)

Today, the Rebecca Lee Society of Women in Medicine is named for Dr. Rebecca Lee Crumpler. So is the Rebecca Lee Pre-Health Society at Syracuse University. Both groups promote diversity in the health professions. No known photo of Rebecca exists, but a medal representing her was created in her honor. In Richmond in 2019, the governor of Virginia declared March 30 to be Rebecca Lee Crumpler Day, celebrating her life of achievement and her contribution to that city's history.

ANN BRADFORD STOKES

Ann Bradford was surely filled with hope as she looked out on the wide, muddy Mississippi River. She had been born into slavery in the farmlands of middle Tennessee, far from the mighty waters. But in 1861 the Civil War began, and Ann found herself enslaved further south, near the city of Vicksburg, Mississippi. There thousands of African Americans picked cotton for rich white planters. Freedom must have seemed like a distant dream. Then in 1862, Union soldiers and sailors pushed down the Mississippi River on gunboats. The federal troops wanted to capture Vicksburg, where powerful Confederate cannons

Storyteller Marlene Rivero portrays Civil War nurse Ann Stokes. (Courtesy Matt Buckner and Marlene Rivero)

looked down on the river and controlled the passage of ships below. When the Union forces got close, enslaved people fled their plantations. A ship called the Black Hawk picked up Ann and others on the Yazoo River, which flows into the Mississippi. Now, in late 1862, she was sailing on the big river itself, tasting freedom for the first time. She had no idea what lay ahead. But soon Ann would earn a place in history. She was about to become one of the first women in the U.S. Navy.

Ann was born about 1828. Little is known about her parents or her life in Tennessee, except that she never had a chance to go to school and learn to read or write. The farming area where she grew up was near Nashville, the state capital. Politicians there supported slavery and Tennessee's decision to leave the United States. But when Union troops were about to capture the city, the governor and other Confederate leaders fled. That might have been when Ann was moved to Mississippi. Her new home was in the heart of the South. Nearby was the plantation of Jefferson Davis, the president of the Confederacy.

The fight for control of America's greatest river was an important part of the Civil War. Throughout 1862, the Union Navy fought its way south from Illinois on vessels of every kind. There were steamers with giant paddle wheels, ironclads with metal plates, and gunboats loaded with cannons. And there was one unique ship called the Red Rover. It was the Navy's first hospital ship. Soon it would be Ann's new home.

The Red Rover, the U.S. Navy's first hospital ship (Courtesy Library of Congress)

The Red Rover was a 256-foot-long side-wheel steamboat. Built a few years before the Civil War, it hauled people and cargo on the big river. When the war started, the Confederates bought the ship to carry soldiers, and the Red Rover joined the fight against the Union. But a cannonball crashed through the ship's decks and water started pouring in. The captain steered the ship to the shore, and the crew left it there. When Union forces arrived, sailors patched the hole and towed the Red Rover up the river for more repairs.

At the time, the Union was looking for a better way to care for its sick and wounded men as they fought along the river. A hospital ship was the answer, so the Navy rebuilt the Red Rover to do the job. Carpenters added a special laundry, extra bathrooms, and an elevator to carry the injured. An operating room was prepared, and a cold storage locker was built to hold 300 tons of ice. "I wish you could see our hospital boat," wrote one Navy officer when the work was done. "She is designed to be the most complete thing of the kind that ever floated." Now the Red Rover needed nurses.

When the Civil War began, the governor of Indiana had asked a group of nuns called the Sisters of the Order of the Holy Cross to help in Union hospitals. The sisters agreed, and when the Red Rover was ready, three of them joined its medical team. Some African American women also came on board and started helping out. They had escaped slavery and probably had experience delivering babies. This was the first time women had ever joined the Navy or served as nurses on a Navy ship. Around Christmas in 1862, the Red Rover sailed south toward Vicksburg. It met the Black Hawk at the mouth of the Yazoo River. On New Year's Day, Ann joined the Navy and was assigned to the Red Rover. At first, she was listed on the ship's roster as a "contraband," the label given to freed people during the war. Later she would become a nurse.

Illustration of the battle of Fort Hindman (Courtesy Library of Congress)

Tough times lay ahead for the hospital ship. Within a couple of weeks, Union forces attacked Fort Hindman, a Rebel fort on the river. Hundreds of men were wounded. Many were taken to the Red Rover for care. About the same time, a winter storm hit. The crew stayed busy clearing snow, caring for the injured, and burying soldiers who died. A week later, during another battle, two shells smashed into the Red Rover and passed through its hospital ward. Somehow nobody was hurt.

A magazine illustration of the hospital deck of the Red Rover (Courtesy Library of Congress)

After that, the ship mostly stayed anchored near Vicksburg as Union soldiers tried to capture the fortress city. At least once, though, the Red Rover cruised over to the Jefferson Davis plantation, which the Confederate president had abandoned. There they gathered chickens, ducks, and eggs to feed the wounded. On the Fourth of July 1863, the Union forces finally captured Vicksburg. Almost 30,000 Confederates surrendered. It was a turning point in the war. Now Union ships could sail all along the Mississippi River, and the Confederacy was cut in half.

The Red Rover still had a lot to do, though. Ann and the rest of the crew traveled up and down the long river, caring for the injured and carrying them to hospitals on land. The ship spent the winter of 1863-64 being repaired at the big Union shipyard in Mound City, Illinois. Then in April, it cruised south to help the survivors of one of the war's most terrible incidents.

Fort Pillow had been built by the Confederates overlooking the Mississippi River. Union forces captured it in 1862, and two years later, about 600 federal soldiers were living there. Half of them were African American. On April 12, 1864, about 2,000 Rebel cavalrymen surrounded the fort and attacked. The Union commander was killed, and the rest of the soldiers surrendered.

But the Confederates refused to take the Black soldiers prisoner. Instead, the Rebels kept killing the African Americans. In the end, more than 200 Union soldiers were dead and more than 100 were wounded. The Red Rover arrived the next day and took some of the injured soldiers on board.

People in the North were outraged when they heard the news from Fort Pillow. Ann and the other African Americans on the hospital ship must have been especially horrified.

An illustration of the Fort Pillow massacre (Courtesy Library of Congress)

Many of the workers on the Red Rover had escaped bondage. In fact, more than half the crew was African American. At first, the women were given jobs doing laundry and working as maids. But some advanced to the rank of nurse. The men often started as "cabin boys" but became carpenters, cooks, and seamen. The freed people built new lives while working on the ship. An example was a 22-year-old man whose cruel plantation name was Goodfer Nothing. He came onto the Red Rover as a contraband but earned the rank of "coal heaver." He also changed his name to Gasper. One of his relatives, Sarah Nothing, joined the Red Rover as a contraband and became a nurse. Ann did many jobs after she came on board, and on June 1, 1864, she, too, was promoted to nurse.

By then, another member of the crew must have been special to her. Gilbert Stokes had escaped slavery near Vicksburg, just as Ann had. He joined the Navy several months after she did, signing on as a "first class cabin boy." Gilbert was no boy, though. He was a 54-year-old man when he enlisted. Ann fell in love with Gilbert, who was promoted to the rank of seaman.

In October 1864, the Red Rover made its last trip on the Mississippi River, then it cruised back to Mound City. It stayed docked there for the rest of the war, still taking care of the sick and wounded. In November, the Navy released Ann and Gilbert from their service. A month later, they got married and started their life together nearby in southern Illinois. Their days as newlyweds did not last long, though. Gilbert had caught a disease while working on the hospital ship, and he could not shake the illness. He died the following year.

Ann remained in southern Illinois and got to know a man named George Bowman. Like Ann, he was from Tennessee. He had two children, George Jr., who was about 6 years old, and a girl, about 4, who also was named Ann. The couple fell in love, and on Christmas Eve, 1866, Ann and George were married. Two of Ann's friends from the Red Rover joined in the ceremony. About a year later, a baby girl was born. They named her Mary. George worked as a farmer, and young George Jr. went to school. He became the first person in his family to learn to read and write.

Mound City National Cemetery marks graves of U.S. Colored Troops. (Courtesy Department of Veterans Affairs)

After the war, the government gave pensions to Union soldiers and sailors who were disabled and to women whose husbands died because of their service. The payments were to help make up for the losses the injured men and widows suffered from the war. Ann tried to get a widow's pension because her husband Gilbert had died of a wartime illness. But because she could not write, she had a hard time making a proper application. Her request was refused. She probably would not have gotten the payments anyway because she had remarried.

Many years later, though, Ann tried again for a pension. She was more than 60 years old by then and was disabled with heart disease and other medical problems. This time, she did not apply as a widow but as someone who had served in the Navy herself. Nothing like that had ever been done. No woman had ever gotten a pension based on her own military service. The man handling her application did not know what to do. He asked a government lawyer if it was OK. The lawyer researched the question. "I cannot find any authority of law for refusing to pension this woman simply because she served as a nurse," he said, "nor is the question of sex mentioned in the law." Ann got her pension, the first woman ever awarded one for her own service in the United States military. The payments were

$12 a month, nearly the same amount that Union soldiers were paid during the war.

But confusion arose again six years later, when Ann got a letter from the government asking for more information. The letter addressed her as "Sir" and wanted to know her "wife's" name. Ann was ready to respond. Although she was more than 65 years old now, she finally had learned how to read and write. Maybe her stepson who had gone to school had taught her. She proudly wrote across the form: "Sir, I am a woman drawing a pension on my own services as a nurse in a hospital." Then she did something she had been unable to do for most of her life. She signed her name: Ann Stokes.

Red Rover medical facility in Illinois (Courtesy Captain James A. Lovell Federal Health Care Center, Department of Veterans Affairs)

Ann died in 1903, most likely near Belknap, Illinois, not far from Mound City, where the Red Rover spent its final days. The ship made history as the Navy's first hospital ship, caring for 2,497 patients during three years of service. Most of that time, more than half of its crew was African American. Its female crew members were the first women enlisted in the U.S. Navy, and its nurses were the origin of the U.S. Navy Nurse Corps. Ann was part of that history. She made history of her own, too, by being the first woman to get a pension for her own military service. Every year now more than 40,000 Navy recruits -- many of them African Americans and women -- get medical exams at the Red Rover Branch Medical Clinic in Illinois. It is known as the "Gateway to the Navy." Ann's own life is remembered, too, when it is re-enacted on stage by Marlene Rivero, a professional storyteller whose performances honor heroic African American women.

HARRIET TUBMAN

Minty's hair never was combed when she was enslaved in Maryland before the Civil War. "It stood out like a bushel basket," she said. One day when she was a teenager, she was in a village store when another young field hand rushed in. He was being chased by the plantation overseer. The white man burst in and ordered Minty to help him tie up the fugitive. She refused. The young man then darted toward the door. The overseer grabbed a metal weight and threw it at the escaping man. It hit Minty instead. It "broke my skull," she said. The girl was carried away, bleeding and stunned. She sat slumped in a stupor for two days. Finally, she recovered. "I expect that there hair saved my life," she said later. But the injury caused headaches for the rest of her life, and sometimes she would fall asleep suddenly, even while she was talking. Minty began having visions, too, which she felt brought her closer to God. That

Harriet Tubman (Library of Congress)

faith would guide her through many challenges in the years ahead. She would break free of slavery and lead hundreds of others out of bondage.

She would help win the Civil War, working as a nurse, a recruiter, a scout, and a spy. She would fight for African American rights, and for the rights of women, also. She would become one of the most famous women in U.S. history: Harriet Tubman.

Harriet Tubman was born about 1822 on Maryland's Eastern Shore, where her grandmother had been brought in slavery from Africa. That grandmother had a daughter she named Harriet, though everyone called her Rit. When Rit grew up, she married a skilled woodsman named Ben Ross. They had several children, including a daughter named Araminta. Her nickname was Minty. Ben made a cradle for Minty by hollowing out a log from one of the area's sweet gum trees. The child grew up knowing the love of her family but also the brutality of enslavement.

Store where Harriet Tubman was hurt as it stands today in Maryland (Courtesy National Park Service)

When she was just a little girl, she had to wade into freezing water to empty muskrat traps for a white man. She got very sick. Rit nursed her back to health, probably while telling her stories from the Bible and sharing tales of her African heritage. As Minty grew older, she often was whipped, and she carried scars from the beatings. But she was clever, too. One woman beat her almost every day, first thing in the morning. So Minty started wearing extra layers of clothing to protect herself. She pretended that the whippings still hurt terribly. But they were not as bad as before. Minty's family lived in fear of being separated, and one day that nightmare came true. Two of Minty's older sisters were sold. The girls wept as they were led off in chains, never to be seen again. There was nothing that Rit or Ben could do. But later, when Rit learned that the plantation owner planned to sell one of her sons, she hid the boy in the woods so he could not be taken away. Minty was proud of her mother, who found a way to fight back against slavery.

Despite her hardships and head injury, Minty grew into a strong young woman. When she was about 22, she married a free African American man named John Tubman. It was around this time that she changed her name to Harriet, honoring her mother. From then on, she would be known as Harriet Tubman. After the owner of Harriet's plantation died, rumors spread that the new owner would sell Harriet or other family members. She decided to take control of her own fate. "There was one of two things I had a right to, liberty or death," she said. "If I could not have one, I would have the other."

She began planning an escape to the North. But when she told her husband, he said he would not go with her. He was a free man already, and he did not want to leave his home. That did not stop Harriet. When the weather grew cool in 1849, she left. Two of her brothers started out with her, but they gave up. Harriet carried on. She knew how to find the North Star by tracing the "Drinking Gourd" in the sky. She hid during the day and followed the star by night, leaving her life in bondage behind.

THREE HUNDRED DOLLARS REWARD.

RANAWAY from the subscriber on Monday the 17th ult., three negroes, named as follows: HARRY, aged about 19 years, has on one side of his neck a wen, just under the ear, he is of a dark chestnut color, about 5 feet 8 or 9 inches hight; BEN, aged about 25 years, is very quick to speak when spoken to, he is of a chestnut color, about six feet high; MINTY, aged about 27 years, is of a chestnut color, fine looking, and about 5 feet high. One hundred dollars reward will be given for each of the above named negroes, if taken out of the State, and $50 each if taken in the State. They must be lodged in Baltimore, Easton or Cambridge Jail, in Maryland.

ELIZA ANN BRODESS,
Near Bucktown, Dorchester county, Md.
Oct. 3d, 1849.

Newspaper notice offering reward for the capture of Harriet Tubman, then known as Minty, and her brothers (Courtesy National Park Service/Bucktown Village Foundation)

Harriet found friends along the way. For years, people had been helping fugitives make their way to freedom. Many of them were Quakers, members of a religious group who hated slavery. They hid people in houses, cellars, and barns during the day and guided them to the next hiding place at night. The system started about the same time that railroads were being built across the United States. So people called it the Underground Railroad because it could not be seen. Members of the Underground Railroad talked in code. They called themselves "agents." The people who were escaping were called "passengers," and the places they hid were "stations." Guides were called "conductors." When Harriet started her journey, she went to the home of a white woman she knew would help. That woman gave Harriet the names of agents of the Underground Railroad and directions to a station.

As Harriet traveled north, a newspaper advertised a reward for her capture: $50 if she was caught in Maryland, $100 if she was caught outside the state. But Harriet stayed hidden. Finally, she reached Pennsylvania, where slavery was banned. "When I found I had crossed that line, I looked at my hands to see if I was the same person," she said. "There was such a glory over everything; the sun came like gold through the trees, and over the fields, and I felt like I was in Heaven."

Harriet found work in Philadelphia, where leaders of the Underground

Railroad lived. But she worried about her family back in Maryland. One day she got word that a niece named Kessiah and her two children were about to be sold. Harriet knew she had to do something. But the danger was greater than ever. Since her escape, the government had passed the Fugitive Slave Law, which meant that enslaved people who escaped to the North could be captured and sent back to slavery in the South. Despite the risk, Harriet returned to Maryland. Just as Kessiah and her children were about to be sold, they managed to sneak away with Kessiah's husband in a small boat. They met up with Harriet, and she guided them from hiding place to hiding place until they reached freedom. Harriet was overjoyed. She had become a conductor on the Underground Railroad.

Engraving of enslaved people fleeing with the help of the Underground Railroad in the 1850s (Courtesy Internet Archive Book Image/Wikimedia Commons)

In 1851, Harriet went on a second rescue mission, bringing back a brother and two other men. Later that year she made a third trip, this time to a part of Maryland where she was well known. She wanted to bring her husband away. But she found out that he had taken up with another woman and still did not want to leave. Harriet was heartbroken, but she did not let her sadness overwhelm her. She committed herself to helping as many people as she could. She gathered a group of 11 fugitives, including another brother, and led them away. This time they traveled all the way to Canada, beyond the reach of the Fugitive Slave Law. After that, Harriet made one or two trips to Maryland every year, leading more people to freedom. She traveled during the winter when the nights were long. Her reputation grew. She became known as "Moses," because like Moses in the Bible, she led her people to the Promised Land.

Harriet was daring. One time she had to pass through a dangerous town in broad daylight. She put a bonnet over her head and carried two live chickens. When a white man she knew approached, she pulled on the legs of the chickens. They squawked and fluttered. Harriet hid her face, and the man, distracted by the beating wings, passed by without recognizing her. Another time she was on a train when a white man sat nearby. She picked up a newspaper and pretended to read. The man knew that Harriet Tubman could not read, so he paid no attention to her.

Harriet dreamed of reuniting her whole family. Her parents, Ben and Rit, had been given their freedom. But they still lived in Maryland, where they were helping other people escape slavery. She feared they might be arrested, but they were too old to walk all the way to the North. Harriet built a crude wagon out of a couple of wheels and boards. Night after night, Rit and Ben sat on the boards as an old horse led by Harriet pulled the wagon to safety.

Harriet became famous for her work as an Underground Railroad conductor.

Harriet Tubman (Courtesy Library of Congress)

Abolitionists asked her to speak at gatherings. Although she could not read or write, she was a wonderful storyteller. She made people laugh and cry as she shared stories about her life. She had a beautiful singing voice, too, and added songs to her talks, explaining how the songs carried hidden messages. One song she sang was: "Oh go down, Moses / Way down into Egypt land / Tell old Pharaoh, / Let my people go."

Harriet became friends with some of the leading abolitionists in the country. One was William Seward, who was a United States senator from New York. He admired Harriet's work and sold her a seven-acre farm with a house and a barn by his hometown of Auburn, New York. He made her a special deal, charging just $25 up front then $10 every three months. This became Harriet's home. Another famous abolitionist she met was Frederick

Douglass, who, like Harriet, had escaped from slavery in Maryland. He connected her with John Brown, a man who hated slavery so much he wanted to lead the enslaved people in a revolt. He made plans to capture weapons the government had stored in Virginia, and Harriet helped him with the planning. Brown called her "General Tubman." But when the time came to make the raid in Virginia, Harriet could not go. That was for the best because Brown's attack failed. He was captured, put on trial, and sentenced to death. Afterward Harriet said she believed his death was a sign that the day of liberation was coming. "When I think of all the groans and tears and prayers I've heard on plantations and remember that God is a prayer-hearing God, I feel that His time is drawing near," she said.

A painting of John Brown (Courtesy Library of Congress)

After John Brown's death, Harriet fought slavery more fiercely than ever. She heard about a man who had escaped to the North but had been captured in New York. He was in danger of being returned to bondage. She disguised herself as an old woman and went to where the man was being held. When police tried to take him away, Harriet grabbed one of the policemen. Her struggles excited a crowd outside, and people rushed to free the captive. The man got away for a few minutes but was recaptured. As rescuers tried again, officers started shooting. Bullets were "whistling past" when Harriet finally hustled the man away. She was bruised and cut, and her clothes were torn. But the man was safe. The rescue made news across the country.

A few months later, Abraham Lincoln was elected president, and the following spring, the Civil War began. Union forces soon attacked the coast of the Confederacy and captured the Sea Islands of South Carolina and Georgia. Harriet was asked to go to the Sea Islands to help the freed people. They had little clothing and not much to eat. Many were sick with diseases such as smallpox and dysentery. Harriet knew a lot about healing.

She had learned from her mother how to use plants to treat illnesses. She boiled cranesbill herbs and lily roots to make a brew that reduced fevers. She also baked pies and brewed root beer, which she sold to cover her expenses. When she had extra money, she gave it to the needy.

Freed people on the Sea Islands (Courtesy Library of Congress)

Union officers knew of Harriet's work with the Underground Railroad. They asked her to use her talents to help fight the Confederates. Harriet organized a team of African American spies to gather information behind enemy lines. The secrets she learned led to one of her boldest adventures. On the night of June 2, 1863, Harriet guided three Union gunboats loaded with African American soldiers up a river in South Carolina. They were going to raid Rebel plantations. In the darkness, Harriet directed the boats past explosives planted in the river. When she found places to land, the soldiers rushed ashore to burn houses, barns, and mills and to seize rice, cotton, and farm animals.

The boats blew whistles to signal to the enslaved people that rescue had arrived. Men, women, and children ran to the riverbank, ignoring plantation owners who tried to stop them. When the crush of people began to cause a panic, Harriet started singing. The crowd joined in, singing and clapping, and growing calmer. The fugitives brought what belongings they could carry. One woman had a pail of hot cooked rice on her head. Another brought along a pig she named after the Confederate president, Jefferson Davis. "I never saw such a sight," Harriet said. "Sometimes the women would come with twins hanging around their necks." More than 750 African Americans escaped slavery that night, and more than 100 of them joined the Union Army. The raid made Harriet more famous. It also showed leaders in the North how valuable Black soldiers could be.

Illustration of Harriet Tubman's river raid (Courtesy Library of Congress)

Not long after that, a group of Black soldiers proved their courage once and for all. This was the 54th Massachusetts Infantry, which included the sons of African American leaders such as Harriet's friend Frederick Douglass. The regiment was assigned to attack Fort Wagner outside Charleston, South Carolina. The morning of the attack, Harriet made breakfast for the commander, Colonel Robert Shaw. The Black troops fought bravely, but Fort Wagner was impossible to capture. Shaw was killed in the fight, and 272 of the soldiers also were lost.

After the battle, Harriet served as a nurse, going to the hospital every morning to care for the wounded. She would get a sponge and put a big chunk of ice in a basin "Then I'd begin to bathe their wounds," she said. "By the time I'd bathed off three or four, the fire and heat would have melted the ice and made the water warm, and it would be as red as clear blood. Then I'd go and get more ice."

Near the end of the war, Harriet left the Sea Islands and went to Virginia to help the freed people there. That was where she heard that President

Lincoln had been killed. The news hit her especially hard. William Seward, the friend who had provided her with a house, was injured. The same plotters who killed Lincoln had attacked Seward, too. Happily, he survived his wounds. Harriet returned to her home in Auburn, New York, a few months later.

On the trip back, she was reminded of the racism African Americans faced even though the war was over. She was riding on a train when the conductor ordered her to move to a different car because she was Black. She said no. The man tried to drag her away, but she held on. Two other men helped him, and when they forced her out of the car, they broke her arm and hurt her shoulder and ribs. She had to rest and recover in New York City before she could complete her journey.

Secretary of State William Seward (Courtesy Library of Congress)

Soon Harriet heard more disturbing news. In 1867, she learned that her husband, John Tubman, had been shot and killed by a white man. The man was arrested and put on trial. But he claimed self-defense, and an all-white jury found him not guilty. Although Harriet had not been with her husband for many years, his death and the unfairness of the trial left her feeling sad and angry.

Around the same time, though, another man came into her life. His name was Nelson Davis. Nelson had escaped slavery and during the war had joined an African American regiment that was sent to the Sea Islands. There he met Harriet. After the war, he made his way to her New York home. He was sick then with tuberculosis, and he stayed with her while he recovered. Over the next year and a half, he grew stronger, and so did their relationship. They got married in 1869 in Auburn's Central Presbyterian Church. Harriet's parents were there for the big church wedding along with other family members and leaders of the community. A few years after they were married, Harriet and Nelson adopted a girl. They called her Gertie.

Harriet kept her home in Auburn open to people in need. She dreamed of building a special place for older African Americans to live. But getting money was a struggle. Friends tried to help. One was Sarah Hopkins Bradford. She spent hours talking to Harriet and other people about her achievements, and she wrote a book called *Scenes in the Life of Harriet*

Tubman. The book sold for a dollar a copy, and Harriet earned more than $1,200. But a few years later, two wicked men came to Auburn and took advantage of her need to raise money. They told her that they had gold that had been buried by a wealthy planter in South Carolina and had been dug up after the war. They offered to sell it to her. But when Harriet showed up, they tied her up and took her money. The crime outraged her friends.

Harriet had been paid almost nothing for her work during the war. After it was over, she asked for payment. But she was turned down because she did not have careful records of what she had done. Some friends tried to get the government to make a special payment to her. But that failed, as well. Nelson earned some money by farming and running a brick-making business. But in 1888 he grew sicker again and died.

Harriet Tubman, her daughter Gertie, and her husband Nelson Davis (Courtesy New York Public Library)

Harriet was in great need. The government began providing pensions to the widows of soldiers who were in the Union Army. Because Nelson had served, Harriet applied for the monthly payments. Again, problems with records slowed things down. But in 1892, when she was about 70 years old, the government finally awarded Harriet a pension of $8 a month. That was little more than half of what soldiers were paid when they were in the Union Army, and Harriet had recruited more than 100 soldiers to the cause. Seven years later, though, friends in the government got her pension raised to $20 a month.

Harriet never gave up on her dream of opening a home for old and needy Black Americans. When she got the chance, she borrowed some money and bought more land and another building near her home for that purpose. In 1903, when she was about 80 years old, she donated the building to the AME Zion Church. Over the next five years, the church raised more money to prepare the home. In 1908, the Harriet Tubman Home for Aged and Invalid Negroes opened. Harriet was the guest of honor at the ceremony.

During the final years of her life, Harriet's fame spread far and wide. The queen of England sent her a beautiful shawl and silver medal and invited her to visit, an invitation Harriet had to turn down. She spent much of her time now speaking out for women's rights. African American men had been given the right to vote when the 15th Amendment to the Constitution passed in 1870. But women -- white and African American – still were not allowed to vote. Harriet went to many rallies, representing the voice of Black women. She became known as "Mother Tubman." At one conference, she was introduced by Susan B. Anthony, the famous women's rights leader. The two stood together on the stage holding hands as the crowd cheered. During her talk, Harriet made her famous statement: "I was a conductor for the Underground Railroad for eight years, and I can say what most conductors can't say -- I never ran my train off the track and I never lost a passenger."

Illustration of Harriet Tubman from Scenes in the Life of Harriet Tubman by Sarah H. Bradford (Courtesy Tennessee State Library) and Archives)

Harriet Tubman personally led about 70 enslaved people to freedom, and she taught many others how to escape. During the Civil War, she helped free hundreds more people from bondage. She died on March 10, 1913, at the age of about 91. She was buried with military honors in a cemetery near her Auburn home. Well known African American and white people came to mourn her. Today, the Harriet Tubman Home is preserved as a museum. Schools and streets across the United States are named for her, and statues of her stand in several cities. Her face has been on a U.S. postage stamp, and the government has made plans to put her picture on the $20 bill.

Harriet Tubman in 1911 (Courtesy Library of Congress)

SALLIE DAFFIN

Cecilia Daffin was a businesswoman. At a time when many African Americans in Philadelphia worked as servants, she was an independent dressmaker. Her daughters, Harriet and Sallie, helped with the business. Harriet, the oldest, became a skilled dressmaker like her mother. Sallie left school when she was 11 and started learning the dress-making trade, too. But she had other dreams. Sallie loved learning, and she wanted to share what she learned. "Her thoughts were upon books and work, not the work of the needle, but of the brain and heart," said a leader of the family's African Methodist Episcopal Church. Sallie Daffin was determined to become a teacher.

Students at Cheyney University used this silhouette to represent Sallie Daffin in a history project about the Institute for Colored Youth's first students. No picture of Sallie is known to exist. (Courtesy Wikimedia Commons)

The AME church was a central part of Sallie's life. The church had been started in Philadelphia many years earlier by a man named Richard Allen. He had first heard the words of the Bible in a clearing in a forest because in those days enslaved people like him had to gather in secret. After he grew up and gained his freedom, he became a minister. He was a powerful speaker, and a

Portrait of Richard Allen, founder of the African Methodist Episcopal Church (Courtesy Library of Congress)

mixed-race church in Philadelphia invited him to preach. But after more African Americans came to hear his sermons, a balcony was built to segregate the Black worshippers. One day, when Reverend Allen and a friend arrived, they kneeled to pray in a part of the church reserved for white people. A man rushed over and tried to drag them out. "Wait until the prayer is over," the friend said, then he and Reverend Allen led many of the African Americans out, never to return. They started their own church. The African Methodist Episcopal Church would grow to include millions of Black Americans, including the Daffins.

Sallie was born in 1837. In those years before the Civil War, Philadelphia did not have good public schools for Black children. The white teachers often were not enthusiastic. Yet the city refused to hire African American teachers. Many parents simply taught their children at home. Some Quakers, members of the religious group that had founded Philadelphia, wanted to help. They started a school to train African American teachers. The Institute for Colored Youth opened in 1852, when Sallie was a teenager. It was the nation's first college for African Americans. The school hired the finest Black educators, and they set high standards. Students learned advanced math, chemistry, literature, and how to read in Latin and Greek. Sallie enrolled just a few years after the Institute opened, and soon she was a star. She earned a top math prize and won a contest by writing an essay about alcohol abuse. When she graduated in 1860, she thought about traveling to Africa to work as a missionary. But Sallie decided to stay in the United States and bring the light of literacy to other African American children.

Memorial portrays the Institute for Colored Youth (Courtesy Mark Jason Dominus/CC By SA)

Black Americans who fled enslavement in Virginia (Courtesy Library of Congress)

She went into the world with "torch in hand," said one AME church leader. Over the next few years, Sallie taught in Pennsylvania and in nearby states, becoming a better and better teacher. In Wilmington, Delaware, parents "almost idolized" her, said one man. They did everything they could to keep her there. But by then, the Civil War had begun. Sallie heard about the hardships of the families fleeing slavery. Their struggles cried out to her. "They are my people," she said. So she applied to the American Missionary Association, which was sending teachers to the help the freed people. Her "soul found no rest till she went to the South," said one newspaper writer. In March 1864, the AMA sent Sallie to Norfolk, Virginia. There she would carry the torch of knowledge to children who had been enslaved.

Norfolk was at the mouth of the James River, where the English had first settled at Jamestown in 1607, and where people from Africa were first brought in chains to America. On the other side of the wide body of water was Fort Monroe, a mighty fortress guarding the waterways that led to both Richmond, Virginia, and Washington, D.C. When the Civil War began in 1861, the federal government rushed thousands of troops to Fort Monroe to make sure it would stay in Union hands. The day that Virginia joined the Confederacy, three enslaved men fled to Fort Monroe and asked for protection. The commander was Major General Benjamin Butler. When a Rebel officer demanded that the three men be returned, Butler refused. He said that, since the Southerners treated the men as property, he would treat them as "contraband," which means captured enemy property. The name stuck. For the rest of the Civil War, people who escaped slavery and reached Union lines were called "contrabands." Soon word spread, and dozens of men, women, and children escaped to Fort Monroe every day. It became known as Freedom's Fortress.

The following year, Union forces attacked across the mouth of the James River and captured the city of Norfolk. More enslaved people were freed, and thousands fled to the city. When President Abraham Lincoln's Emancipation Proclamation took effect, 4,000 Black Americans paraded down the main streets of Norfolk, cheering and waving flags. But daily life was hard there. Two to three women and children starved to death every day, and men stole bread to feed their families. The freed people needed clothing, too. One woman arrived with eight children wearing nothing but rags held together with string. When Sallie got to Norfolk, she found her students eager to learn. "Although there is much physical suffering, it is seldom we hear any murmuring," she wrote in a

Two men who escaped slavery in tattered clothes (Courtesy Library of Congress)

letter. But she asked the people back home to send clothes. "There is many a garment cast aside by our friends of the North as useless, which ... would bring joy and gladness to many hearts," she wrote.

Sallie loved teaching. She taught children during the day and adults in the evening. She also taught Sunday school, helping children memorize the Ten Commandments and other parts of the Bible. She and three other women set up a school that was taught only by African Americans, which was considered a bold experiment at the time. But her duties went beyond teaching. When pupils were sick, she went to their homes to care for them. She also was a leader of the Ladies' Soldiers' Relief Association. That meant nursing sick and wounded African American soldiers and collecting supplies for them.

"Could you, dear friends," she wrote, "stand around the couches of the ill and dying … you would not for a moment hesitate to contribute." She described the day a ship landed carrying wounded soldiers: "The groans and screams of some of the poor fellows, who were being moved on stretchers to the ambulances, were truly heart-rending. Some of them were wounded in the leg, some in the arm, others in the body … One poor man had both eyes shot out."

Sergeant Major Thomas R. Hawkins (Courtesy Library of Congress)

Among the Black soldiers was Sergeant Major Thomas R. Hawkins. He had joined the Army in Philadelphia, and Sallie knew him. He was hurt in the shoulder, thigh, and foot. But Hawkins spoke cheerfully despite his pain. "I am glad I was in this battle," he said. "I would not have missed it for anything." Hawkins later was awarded the Medal of Honor, the nation's highest award for bravery.

Just as the war ended in April 1865, the American Missionary Association moved Sallie further south, to Wilmington, North Carolina. Soon news arrived that President Lincoln had been killed. The Black community was stunned. "Tears of grief and anguish burst forth," Sallie remembered. But the white Southerners were not unhappy. They were bitter at losing the war and their power. They harassed and robbed the freed people. "One or two have been killed," Sallie wrote. African American troops finally arrived and brought order to the city.

Sallie faced racism in her personal life, too. The superintendent of schools, Reverend Samuel Ashley, thought she should stay with an African American family instead of in a house with white teachers. He knew Black teachers were needed in the South, but he was afraid of local reaction. "It does not seem to me to be wise to send them in … with white teachers," he said. But Sallie refused to be discriminated against. Despite the racial tension in Wilmington, she felt good about what she was doing. "As there will be much work to be done … and as my health is excellent," she wrote, "I think I shall remain here for some time yet, unless I am ordered away."

Eventually, the AMA did give Sallie jobs teaching elsewhere. She spent time in Maryland, where her teaching was hampered by a shortage of books. That did not stop her. Sallie created lessons using what already was in her classroom – namely her students – and taught them about the bones in the human body. In Washington, D.C., she was in charge of a school for girls that was run in the basement of a church. In Arlington, Virginia, she worked near the grand home that had once belonged to Robert E. Lee, the Confederate general. Now from the top of that building "proudly waves the symbol of Freedom - The glorious Stars and Stripes," Sallie wrote. She had so many students in Arlington that she had to split them into two classes, one in the morning and one in the afternoon.

Displaced African Americans gather with books at the Freedmen's Village in Arlington. (Courtesy Library of Congress)

Despite her hard work and experience, though, she was treated with disrespect by a white teacher. The woman pressured Sallie into handling the beginning students even though she was better qualified to teach the advanced class. The teacher was "bitter and cruel" during mealtimes and every chance she got, Sallie said. Eventually, Sallie resigned. The freed people of Arlington pleaded for her to return for the next school year. She wanted to stay but ended up parting ways with the American Missionary Association.

Sallie would not give up teaching in the South, though. Three years after the war ended, some folks in Philadelphia started a new group to help the freed people. Its leader was Henry H. Garnet, an abolitionist minister who was

Henry Highland Garnet (Courtesy National Portrait Gallery)

the first African American to speak to the United States Congress. Garnet believed that white teachers did not understand Black men. He wanted Black teachers to instruct the freed people. His Garnet League started sending teachers to the South, and Sallie was hired to start a school in Clinton, Tennessee.

Things went well at first. Neighbors pitched in to build a schoolhouse that also served as a church. Supporters donated gifts, and even though it was April, Sallie decided to have a Christmas party. Students arrived and found presents under a Christmas tree. It was the first Christmas tree some of them had ever seen. The school thrived. At the end of the first year, the citizens of Clinton met and voted to thank Sallie for her "untiring, able and devoted efforts." They asked her to come back for the next school year, and she did. In 1869, Sallie reported that she had 64 pupils who were very well behaved. "We have been teaching here a year and have yet to punish a single scholar," she wrote.

But many white Southerners hated seeing the school succeed. Since the end of the war, some former Confederates had tried to spread terror among the freed people. In Memphis, Tennessee, white rioters burned 12 African American schools. In another part of Tennessee, former Rebel soldiers formed a secret hate group, the Ku Klux Klan. Clinton was in East Tennessee, a part of the state where feelings about slavery had been mixed. Many white people had supported the Union, but others had backed the Confederacy.

On March 4, 1869, Ulysses S. Grant became president of the United States. Grant was the general who had led the North to victory in the Civil War. Sallie's school raised the American flag in celebration. On the blackboard, she wrote: "Three Cheers for U.S. Grant, President of the U. States." That weekend, white terrorists sneaked into the school and used Bibles and other books to build a fire. The school burned to the ground. Sallie and her Sunday school pupils arrived to find only "a smoldering heap of ashes," she reported. But the attack did not put an end to the school. Sympathetic white people in Clinton held a meeting and criticized the "cowardly act."

They raised money and made plans to rebuild the school. They also invited the African American students to continue their lessons in a Baptist Church where white people worshipped. "The day school has not been stopped for a single hour," Sallie wrote. "What seemed so great a misfortune at first, has been productive of good results."

Illustration of a Tennessee mob burning an African American schoolhouse after the Civil War (Courtesy Library of Congress)

Sallie continued teaching in Tennessee until 1870, when she became the principal of a public school for Black children in Washington, D.C. She stayed there for many years. For a while she lived with her mother, and in 1880, she was living with her sister, Harriet. Just two doors down the street lived Charlotte Forten Grimke´. Charlotte and Sallie were born the same year in Philadelphia, so maybe they knew each other as girls. Growing up, they both were education trailblazers. During the Civil War, they worked as teachers and as nurses. As neighbors, they certainly had a lot to talk about.

Sallie was still in Washington in 1886, when she turned 49 years old. But after that, she disappears from history. No records have been found that tell what else she did in her remarkable life or when and where she died. No pictures of her have been discovered. Sallie Daffin is mostly remembered today by scholars who study her letters to understand what life was like for the brave African Americans women who worked to heal and teach the struggling people of the South who were freed by the Civil War.

CIVIL WAR MEDICINE

Before the Civil War, nursing was not the profession it is today. At home, women cared for family members who were sick or hurt. They used traditional cures learned from mothers, aunts, and grandmothers. But not many women worked in hospitals, and there were no nursing schools. Men handled nursing duties in the military. Women were considered too frail for the job.

When the war came, that attitude started to change. Men were needed as soldiers, and women wanted to do what they could to help. Some were inspired by a British woman named Florence Nightingale. A few years before the Civil War, she had helped organize hospitals during a terrible war between Britain and Russia. A newspaper reported that she would walk from bed to bed at night

Florence Nightingale tending patients (Courtesy CC by 4.0)

with a light in her hand, checking on wounded soldiers. She became famous as the Lady with the Lamp and was admired for her dedication. Many courageous American women were determined to follow in her footsteps.

Medicine was very different then. Germs had not been discovered, so health care workers did not know how to control the spread of disease and infection. Doctors had very few medicines to use, and surgery was crude. Often when a soldier was wounded in an arm or a leg, a surgeon cut off the limb. Otherwise the wound would get infected and likely kill the soldier. Three quarters of all the operations done during the Civil War were amputations.

Getting sick was an even greater danger than being wounded in battle. Twice as many soldiers died of sickness as died of wounds. Common illnesses were:

- Diarrhea or dysentery -- These illnesses happened when germs in unclean food or water attacked soldiers' bowels. Out of every ten soldiers, about seven of them suffered this kind of illness each year.

- Malaria -- Mosquitos spread this disease, which caused a high fever. A quarter of the Union soldiers who needed medical help had malaria.

- Typhoid fever -- Flies, as well as dirty food and water, spread this deadly infection. About 75,000 Union soldiers caught typhoid fever. Washington, D.C., was hit hard. One person who died was President Abraham Lincoln's 11-year-old son Willie.

- Smallpox -- This virus spread from person to person. It caused a fever and a bad rash that killed patients or left them scarred. Doctors knew that vaccination could prevent smallpox. But many people could not get the vaccine. African Americans especially were in danger, and they caught smallpox seven times as often as white people did.

- Tuberculosis -- A germ that can float in the air caused this disease, also called TB or consumption. It made people cough, so it spread easily in crowded army and refugee camps.

- Scurvy -- A lack of vitamin C caused this illness. During the war, soldiers mostly ate dried biscuits and salted beef or pork. They got few fruits and vegetables, which contained vitamin C. Scurvy left soldiers weak and in pain. Getting healthy food to patients was an important job for nurses.

- Cholera -- This deadly disease was caused by germs getting into water and food. Epidemics of cholera swept through the United States during the 1800s, including right after the Civil War in 1866.

Sickness hit African American soldiers especially hard. They died of illness more than twice as often as white soldiers did. Almost one out of every five Black soldiers died of disease.

African American refugees crossing the Rappahannock River in Virginia (Timothy O'Sullivan photograph courtesy Library of Congress)

Staying healthy was a struggle for all the people who escaped slavery. Many had little shelter or clothing as they tried to build new lives. They gathered in camps that had unsafe food and water. Between 1862 and 1870, about a million African American refugees got sick or died. Just one outbreak of smallpox in Washington, D.C., killed at least 60,000 freed people. Often white health care workers did not make helping African Americans a top priority. Aid from other Black Americans was important.

There were a few African American doctors. The best known was Dr. Alexander Augusta. He grew up in Virginia and secretly learned to read and write while working as a barber. He wanted to be a doctor but was not allowed into a medical school in the United States. So he went to Canada to study medicine. When the Civil War began, he volunteered for the Union Army, and President Lincoln made him a surgeon assigned to helping Black soldiers.

During the war, Freedmen's Hospital was set up in Washington, D.C., to care for African American refugees. Dr. Augusta was put in charge. He hired other Black Americans to help. After the war, Freedmen's Hospital became part of Howard University. Dr. Augusta was the first African American to run a hospital and the first to teach at a medical school. The hospital continues to operate to this day as Howard University Hospital, a major teaching hospital in the nation's capital.

Dr. Alexander Augusta (Courtesy National Library of Medicine)

NURSES TIMELINE

1797 -- Sojourner Truth is born in Ulster County, New York.

1822 -- Harriet Tubman is born about this time in Dorchester County, Maryland.

1826 -- Sojourner Truth frees herself.

1828 -- Ann Bradford Stokes is born about this time in Rutherford County, Tennessee.

1831 -- Rebecca Lee Crumpler is born in Christiana, Delaware.

1837 -- Charlotte Forten Grimke´ and Sarah L. "Sallie" Daffin are both born in Philadelphia, Pennsylvania.

1848 -- Susie King Taylor is born in Liberty County, Georgia.

1849 -- Harriet Tubman escapes from slavery.

1850 -- Fugitive Slave Act becomes law. The *Narrative of Sojourner Truth* is published. Harriet Tubman becomes an Underground Railroad conductor.

An 1850s illustration showing men being hunted down under the Fugitive Slave Law (Courtesy Library of Congress)

1855 -- Susie King Taylor moves to Savannah, Georgia, and begins learning to read and write in a secret school.

1856 -- Charlotte Forten Grimke´ becomes the first African American graduate of Salem Normal School in Massachusetts.

1860 -- Abraham Lincoln is elected president of the United States. Sallie Daffin graduates from the Institute for Colored Youth in Philadelphia.

April 1861 – The Civil War begins when Confederates in South Carolina bombard Fort Sumter in Charleston harbor.

Illustration of the bombardment of Fort Sumter at the start of the Civil War (Courtesy Library of Congress)

1862 -- Charlotte Forten Grimke´ becomes the first African American to volunteer to go south to teach freed people. She becomes a teacher and nurse in the Sea Islands. Susie King Taylor escapes slavery and begins teaching and nursing in the Sea Islands, too. Harriet Tubman arrives there, also, and works as a nurse and scout.

January 1, 1863 – The Emancipation Proclamation ending slavery in Rebel states takes effect; Ann Bradford Stokes enlists in the U.S. Navy.

June 2-3, 1863 -- Harriet Tubman guides gunboats and African American soldiers on a raid in South Carolina that frees 750 enslaved people.

July 18, 1863 – The 54th Massachusetts Infantry Regiment attacks Fort Wagner outside Charleston. Hundreds of the African American soldiers are killed. Charlotte Forten Grimke´, Susie King Taylor, and Harriet Tubman help care for the wounded.

1864 -- Rebecca Lee Crumpler becomes the first African American woman to earn a medical degree. Sojourner Truth moves to Washington, D.C., to help freed people and fights to integrate the city's streetcars. Sallie Daffin begins working in Norfolk, Virginia, as a teacher and nurse.

April 1865 -- The Civil War ends after the fall of Richmond, Virginia. President Lincoln is killed.

Engraving depicting Confederate surrender at the
end of Civil War (Courtesy Wikimedia Commons)

1866 -- Rebecca Lee Crumpler moves to Richmond to help freed people.

1869 -- Sallie Daffin's schoolhouse in Tennessee is burned by racists. White
and African American people in the community rebuild the school.

1883 -- Sojourner Truth dies in Battle Creek, Michigan, at the age of 86; Dr.
Rebecca Lee Crumpler's *Book of Medical Discourses* is published, one of the
first medical texts by an African American.

1886 – The last known record of Sallie Daffin shows her living in
Washington, D.C. She is 49.

1890 -- Ann Bradford Stokes becomes the first woman to receive a pension
for her own U.S. military service.

1894 -- Rebecca Lee Crumpler dies in Boston, Massachusetts, at the age of
64.

1902 -- Susie King Taylor publishes *Reminiscences of My Life in Camp,* the only
account of Civil War military service by an African American woman.

1903 -- Ann Bradford Stokes dies in southern Illinois at the age of about
75.

1912 -- Susie King Taylor dies in Boston at the age of 64.

1913 -- Harriet Tubman dies in Auburn, New York, at the age of about 90.

1914 -- Charlotte Forten Grimke´ dies in Washington, D.C., at the age of
76.

1953 -- *The Journal of Charlotte L. Forten* is published.

THINGS TO KNOW ABOUT

1st South Carolina Volunteers -- The first African American Army unit of the Civil War. It was formed in 1862 of men who escaped enslavement.

13th Amendment -- The change to the Constitution that went into effect in 1865, ending slavery in the United States.

14th Amendment – The 1868 change to the Constitution that gave citizenship rights to people who had been enslaved.

15th Amendment -- The 1870 change to the Constitution that gave African American men the right to vote.

54th Massachusetts Infantry -- The most famous African American unit of the Civil War. Its soldiers included two of Frederick Douglass's sons and one of Sojourner Truth's grandsons.

Abolitionist -- Someone who fought to end slavery.

African Methodist Episcopal Church -- The nation's first independent African American church. It originated in 1787.

The resolution passed by Congress proposing the 13th Amendment to the Constitution abolishing slavery in the United States (Courtesy Library of Congress)

American Missionary Association -- An abolitionist church group that started schools and colleges to help people who had been enslaved.

Contrabands - A label given to enslaved people who escaped to the Union

71

side during the war.

Emancipation Proclamation -- President Abraham Lincoln's declaration that all people enslaved in Rebel states were free. It took effect on January 1, 1863.

Fort Monroe - A fort in Virginia that was held by Union forces. It became known as Freedom's Fortress as thousands of enslaved people made their way there.

Fort Pillow -- A fort in Tennessee where Rebel soldiers killed hundreds of African American soldiers who were surrendering.

Freedmen's Bureau -- A United States government office set up to help people who were freed from enslavement by the Civil War.

Fugitive Slave Law -- A law passed in 1850 that said enslaved people who escaped to free states had to be returned to slavery.

Institute for Colored Youth -- The first African American college, started in 1837. It now is called Cheyney University of Pennsylvania.

New England Female Medical College -- The first school in the United States to train women to be doctors. It started in 1848.

Quakers -- A religious group with many members who opposed slavery before the Civil War.

Sea Islands -- Islands along the coasts of Georgia and South Carolina that Union forces captured early in the Civil War.

Underground Railroad -- A secret network of people and hiding places that helped enslaved people escape to freedom in the North before the Civil War.

HISTORICAL FIGURES

Allen, Richard -- The founder of the African Methodist Episcopal Church.

Anthony, Susan B. -- A leader of the fight for women's rights, especially the right to vote.

Augusta, Dr. Alexander – The doctor in charge of Freedmen's Hospital in Washington, and the first African American to teach in a medical school.

Barton, Clara -- A Union nurse. After the war, she started the American Red Cross.

Brown, John -- An abolitionist who led a raid on a weapons storehouse in Virginia before the Civil War. The raid failed and he was hanged.

Frederick Douglass and Susan B. Anthony meet in a sculpture by Pepsy M. Kettavong called "Let's Have Tea" that stands in Rochester, New York. (Photograph courtesy the Carol M. Highsmith Archive, Library of Congress)

Butler, Benjamin -- The Union general in command of Fort Monroe early in the Civil War. When enslaved African Americans fled there in 1861, he would not return them to southern planters, saying they were "contraband," or property seized in war.

Davis, Jefferson -- A Mississippi politician and planter who became president of the Confederate States of America.

Douglass, Frederick -- A man who escaped enslavement and became an abolitionist leader. His book, *Narrative of the Life of Frederick Douglass,* drew many people to the fight against slavery.

Garnet, Henry Highland -- An abolitionist who escaped slavery and become a minister and educator. He was the first African American to speak in the U.S. Capitol.

Garrison, William Lloyd – An abolitionist who published the anti-slavery newspaper *The Liberator.*

Grant, Ulysses S. -- The general who led the Union to victory in the Civil War. Afterward he was elected president of the United States.

Higginson, Thomas -- An abolitionist who became a colonel in the Civil War and led the 1st South Carolina Volunteers.

Lee, Robert E. -- The leading general of the Confederate army.

Lincoln, Abraham -- The president of the United States elected in 1860. He issued the Emancipation Proclamation freeing enslaved people in Rebel states and was killed just a few days after the war ended in April 1865.

Seward, William -- A United States senator who became secretary of state for Abraham Lincoln. He was attacked in the same plot that killed the president.

Shaw, Robert -- The Union colonel who led the 54th Massachusetts Infantry. He was killed in the attack on Fort Wagner.

Stowe, Harriett Beecher -- An abolitionist who wrote a novel called *Uncle Tom's Cabin* before the Civil War. The book told of the lives of enslaved people and showed many people the evils of slavery.

Harriet Beecher Stowe
(Courtesy Library of Congress)

BOOKS BY THE NURSES OR FRIENDS

Bradford, Sarah H. *Harriet Tubman, The Moses of Her People*. Mineola, NY: Dover Publications, 1981.

Crumpler, Rebecca. *A Book of Medical Discourses: in Two Parts*. United States: Forgotten Books.; 2017.

Forten, Charlotte L. *The Journal of Charlotte L. Forten: A young black woman's reactions to the white world of the Civil War era*. New York: Norton, 1981.

Taylor, Susie King. *Reminiscences of My Life in Camp: An African American Woman's Civil War Memoir*. Athens, GA: University of Georgia Press, 2006.

Truth, Sojourner. *Narrative of Sojourner Truth*. New York: Vintage Books, 1993.

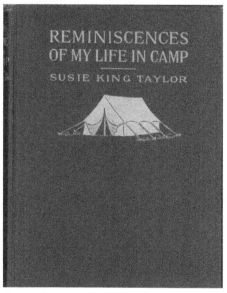

Original edition of Susie King Taylor's book (Courtesy Library of Congress)

PLACES TO VISIT

- African American Museum in Philadelphia, 701 Arch Street Philadelphia, Pennsylvania, https://www.aampmuseum.org/
- Boston African American National Historic Site and Museum of African American History, 46 Joy Street, Beacon Hill, Boston, Massachusetts, https://www.nps.gov/boaf/index.htm and https://www.maah.org/
- Contrabands & Freedmen Memorial Cemetery, 1001 S Washington St, Alexandria, Virginia, https://www.alexandriava.gov/FreedmenMemorial
- Fort Monroe National Monument, 41 Bernard Road, Fort Monroe, Virginia, https://www.nps.gov/fomr/index.htm
- Fort Pulaski National Monument, 101 Fort Pulaski Road, Savannah, Georgia, https://www.nps.gov/fopu/index.htm
- Harriet Tubman Underground Railroad National Historic Park, 4068 Golden Hill Road, Church Creek, Maryland, https://www.nps.gov/hatu/index.htm, and the Harriet Tubman Underground Railroad Byway in Maryland, Delaware and Pennsylvania, https://harriettubmanbyway.org/
- National Museum of African American History and Culture, 1400 Constitution Avenue NW, Washington, D.C., https://nmaahc.si.edu/
- National Museum of Civil War Medicine, 48 E Patrick Street, Frederick, Maryland, https://www.civilwarmed.org/

- National Underground Railroad Museum, 50 E Freedom Way, Cincinnati, Ohio, https://www.freedomcenter.org/
- Statue of Sojourner Truth with Susan B. Anthony and Elizabeth Cady Stanton in Central Park, New York City

Historical marker commemorates Harriet Tubman's work with the Underground Railroad. (Courtesy Maryland Historical Trust)

BIBLIOGRAPHY

Alcott, Louisa May. *Hospital Sketches*. Applewood Books, 1993.

Brackman, Barbara. "Susie King Taylor & her GAR Quilt". *Civil War Quilts. Jan. 11, 2020.* http://civilwarquilts.blogspot.com/2020/01/susie-king-taylor-her-gar-quilt.html.

Bradford, Sarah H. *Harriet, The Moses of Her People*. Geo. R. Lockwood & Son, 1886.

Bradford, Sarah H. *Scenes in the Life of Harriet Tubman*. W.J. Moses, 1869.

Brosnan, AnneMarie. "To educate themselves: southern black teachers in North Carolina's schools for the freedpeople during the Civil War and reconstruction period, 1862–1875". *American Nineteenth Century History*, vol. 20, no. 3, 2019, pp. 231-248.

Buckner, Matt. "Marlene Rivero and Ann Stokes." YouTube portrayal of Ann Stokes by re-enactor Marlene Rivero. Feb. 12, 2013. https://www.youtube.com/watch?v=r2NfOcvnAZs.

Burden, LCDR Tom, MSC, USN (Ret.). "An Overview of US Navy Hospital Ships". *Naval Order of the United States*. Mar. 1, 2017. https://www.navalorder.org/articles/2016/8/28/an-overview-of-hospital-ships.

Butts, Heather, JD, MPH, MA. *African American Medicine in Washington, D.C., Healing the Capital During the Civil War Era*. The History Press, 2014.

"Charlotte Forten". Salem State University.

https://www.salemstate.edu/charlotte-forten.

Clinton, Catherine. *Harriet Tubman, the Road to Freedom*. Little, Brown, 2004.

Condon, Amy Paige. "Pioneering Savannah teacher Susie King Taylor's undertold story comes full circle". *Bluffton Today*. Feb. 20, 2018. https://www.blufftontoday.com/news/2018-02-20/pioneering-savannah-teacher-susie-king-taylor-s-undertold-story-comes-full-circle.

Crumpler, Rebecca. *A Book of Medical Discourses in Two Parts*. Cashman, Keating, 1883.

Cumming, Kate. *The Journal of a Confederate Nurse*. Louisiana State University Press, 1959.

Daffin, Sarah L. "Sallie". *The Christian Recorder*. Various letters including "Tennessee Correspondence", Mar. 13, 1869; "Letter from East Tennessee", Apr. 25, 1868; "Letter from Clinton, Tenn.", Oct. 3, 1868; "Acknowledgement", Sept. 17, 1964; "School burned", Mar. 27, 1869; "From a Philadelphian", Apr. 27, 1867; "An appeal in behalf of the American Missionary Association of New York". Sept. 30, 1965; "Wilmington correspondence". Jun. 19, 1865; "Acknowledgement", Dec. 9, 1865; "Our banner to the breeze in Washington", Sept. 29, 1866; "Letter from Wilmington, N.C.", May 29, 1865.

Dalleo, Peter T. "The Growth of Delaware's antebellum Free African American Community". *A History of African Americans of Delaware and Maryland's Eastern Shore*. University of Delaware. June 27, 1997. http://www1.udel.edu/BlackHistory/antebellum.html.

Davis, Christina Lenore. *The Collective Identities of Women Teachers in Black Schools in the Post-Bellum South*. 2016. The University of Georgia, PhD dissertation. https://getd.libs.uga.edu/pdfs/davis_christina_l_201605_phd.pdf.

Egenes, Karen J. "Nursing during the US Civil War: a movement toward the professionalization of nursing". *Hektoen International*. Winter 2009. https://hekint.org/2017/02/24/nursing-during-the-us-civil-war-a-movement-toward-the-professionalization-of-nursing-2/#:~:text=It%20is%20estimated%20that%20more,experiences%20caring%20for%20loved%20ones.

Forbes, Ella. *African American Women during the Civil War*. Garland, 1998.

Forten, Charlotte. "Life on the Sea Islands (Part I) A young black woman describes her experience teaching freed slaves during the Civil War." *The Atlantic*. May 1864. https://www.theatlantic.com/magazine/archive/1864/05/life-on-the-sea-islands/308758/.

Forten, Charlotte. "Life on the Sea Islands (Part II) A young black woman describes her experience teaching freed slaves during the Civil War." *The Atlantic*. June 1864. https://www.theatlantic.com/magazine/archive/1864/06/life-on-the-sea-islands-continued/308759/.

Forten, Charlotte. *The Journal of Charlotte L. Forten* as edited by Ray Allen Billington. The Dryden Press, 1953.

Gearhart Levy, Renee. "The Truths Behind the Myth of Harriet Tubman". *Maxwell Perspective*. Spring 2008. Maxwell School of Citizenship and Public Affairs. Syracuse University. https://www.maxwell.syr.edu/news/perspective/the-truths-behind-the-myth-of-harriet-tubman/.

Grimké, Charlotte Forten. "Nine Poems by Charlotte Forten Grimké". *Beltway Poetry Quarterly*. http://www.beltwaypoetry.com/grimke-charlotte-forten/.

Groeling, Meg. "Powerful and Determined: Susie King Taylor and Her Image as Seen by Stephen Restelli". *Emerging Civil War*. Feb. 28, 2019. https://emergingcivilwar.com/2019/02/28/powerful-and-determined-susie-king-taylor-and-her-image-as-seen-by-stephen-restelli/.

Gruggs, Patrick. "Riots (1830s and 1840s)". *The Encyclopedia of Greater Philadelphia*. 2015. Rutgers University. https://philadelphiaencyclopedia.org/archive/riots-1830s-and-1840s/.

"Harriet Ross Tubman (1819-1913) timeline". *The African American History of Western New York*. The Circle Association. http://www.math.buffalo.edu/~sww/0history/hwny-tubman.html.

Hatcher, Richard W. III. "First South Carolina Regiment". *South Carolina Encyclopedia*. May 17, 2016.

http://www.scencyclopedia.org/sce/entries/first-south-carolina-regiment/.

Herwick, Edgar B. III. "The 'Doctresses Of Medicine': The World's 1st Female Medical School Was Established In Boston." *WGBH News.* Nov. 4, 2016. https://www.wgbh.org/news/2016/11/04/how-we-live/doctresses-medicine-worlds-1st-female-medical-school-was-established-boston.

"History of the Institute for Colored Youth". *Institute of Colored Youth in the Civil War Era Classes of 1856 to 1864.* https://exhibits.library.villanova.edu/institute-colored-youth/institute-history/.

"History of the U.S. Navy Hospital Ship Red Rover". *Navy Department. Office of the Chief of Naval Operations. Division of Naval History. Ships' History Section.* Sep. 19, 1961. https://archive.org/stream/HISTORYOFU.S.NAVYHOSPITAL SHIPREDROVER/HISTORY+OF+U.+S.+NAVY+HOSPITA L+SHIP+RED+ROVER_djvu.txt.

Humez, Jean M. *Harriet Tubman, The Life and the Life Stories.* The University of Wisconsin Press, 2003.

Intravartolo, Cindy. "St. Mary's Goes to War: The Sisters of the Holy Cross as Civil War Nurses". *Journal of the Illinois State Historical Society*, vol. 107, no. 3-4, fall/winter 2014, pp. 370-391.

King, Lisa Y. "In Search of Women of African Descent Who Served in the Civil War Union Navy". *The Journal of Negro History,* vol. 83, no. 4, autumn 1998, pp. 302-309.

Larson, Kate Clifford. *Bound for the Promised Land: Harriet Tubman, Portrait of an American Hero.* Ballantine, 2004.

Manning, Dr. Chandra. "Smallpox in the Sea Islands: Clara Barton in South Carolina". *Clara Barton Missing Soldiers Office.* Oct. 15, 2017. National Museum of Civil War Medicine. http://www.clarabartonmuseum.org/smallpox/.

Markel, Dr. Harold. "Celebrating Rebecca Lee Crumpler, first African-American woman physician". *PBS News Hour.* Mar. 9, 2016. https://www.pbs.org/newshour/health/celebrating-rebecca-lee-crumpler-first-african-american-physician.

Masur, Kate. "Winning the Right to Ride. How D.C.'s streetcars became an early battleground for post-emancipation civil rights". *Slate*. Dec. 26, 2017. https://slate.com/human-interest/2017/12/black-activists-post-emancipation-battle-for-d-c-s-city-streetcars-one-of-the-first-civil-rights-victories-on-public-transportation.html.

Moore, Emily L. "The unique journal of the USS Red Rover". *Hektoen International*. Spring 2015. https://hekint.org/2017/02/22/the-unique-journal-of-the-uss-red-rover/.

Neal, Anthony W. "Dr. Crumpler: Nation's first African American woman physician". *The Bay City Banner*. Sept. 5, 2012. https://www.baystatebanner.com/2012/09/05/dr-crumpler-nations-first-african-american-woman-physician/.

Newby-Alexander, Cassandra. *The world was all before them: A study of the black community in Norfolk, Virginia, 1861-1884*. 1992. College of William & Mary, PhD dissertation. https://scholarworks.wm.edu/cgi/viewcontent.cgi?article=3733&context=etd.

Oates, Stephen B. *A Woman of Valor, Clara Barton and the Civil War*. The Free Press, 1994.

Painter, Nell Irvin. *Sojourner Truth, A Life, A Symbol*. W.W. Norton and Co., 1996.

Patterson, James Paul. *The cultural reform project of northern teachers of the freed people, 1862-1870*. 2012. University of Iowa, PhD dissertation. https://doi.org/10.17077/etd.ljp4w0ry.

Reilly, Robert F., MD. "Medical and surgical care during the American Civil War, 1861–1865". *Proceedings of Baylor University Medical Center*, vol. 29(2), April 2016, pp. 138-142. https://www.ncbi.nlm.nih.gov/pmc/articles/PMC4790547/.

Richmond Daily Dispatch, multiple articles including "The Mortality Among the Freedmen", Oct. 10, 1866; "Interments from Cholera", Sept. 13, 1866; "Negro Gullibility", Sept. 19, 1866; announcement concerning Freedmen's Bureau rations, Oct. 10, 1866; "The Mortality Among the Freedmen", Oct. 10, 1866; "Cemeteries for Colored People", Oct. 12, 1866; "The Chain Gang", Dec. 7, 1866; "The Negroes to Evacuate Chimborazo by April 1st - An Important Order", Mar. 24, 1866. Reconstructing Virginia. https://reconstructingvirginia.richmond.edu/items/browse?sort_fi

eld=Dublin+Core%2CDate&sort_dir=a&page=11.

Roca, Steven Louis, "Presence and Precedents: The USS Red Rover during the American Civil War, 1861-1865." *Civil War History,* vol. 44, June 1998, pp. 91-100.

Rogers, Seth. "War-Time Letters From Seth Rogers, M.D. Surgeon of the First South Carolina Afterwards the Thirty-third U.S.C.T. 1862-1863". *Florida History Online.* https://www.unf.edu/floridahistoryonline/Projects/Rogers/letters.html.

"Sarah L. Daffin". *The Institute for Colored Youth in the Civil War Era Classes of 1856 to 1864.* https://exhibits.library.villanova.edu/institute-colored-youth/graduates/sarah-sallie-l-daffin.

Schuessler, Jennifer. "Liberation as a Death Sentence." *The New York Times.* June 10, 2012. https://www.nytimes.com/2012/06/11/books/sick-from-freedom-by-jim-downs-about-freed-slaves.html.

Schultz, Jane E. "Race, Gender, and Bureaucracy: Civil War Army Nurses and the Pension Bureau". *Journal of Women's History,* vol. 6, no. 2, summer 1994, pp. 45-69.

Schultz, Jane E. *Women at the Front: Hospital Workers in Civil War America.* University of North Carolina Press, 2004.

Tanner, Benj. T. *An Apology for African Methodism.* Baltimore, 1867. Electronic Edition. https://docsouth.unc.edu/church/tanner/tanner.html.

Taylor, Susie King. *Reminiscences of My Life in Camp with the 33d United States Colored Troops Late 1st S. C. Volunteers.* Documenting the American South. https://docsouth.unc.edu/neh/taylorsu/taylorsu.html.

Taylor, Susie King. *Reminiscences of My Life In Camp, An African American Woman's Civil War Memoir,* with introd. by Catherine Clinton. The University of Georgia Press, 2006.

"The Story of Virginia's Reconstruction". *The Richmond Daily Dispatch 1866 to 1871.* Reconstructing Virginia. https://reconstructingvirginia.richmond.edu/overview.

Truth, Sojourner. *Narrative of Sojourner Truth*. Edited by Margaret Washington. Vintage Books, 1993.

Vermeer, Hunter. "Propriety Meets Necessity: Female Nursing in the Civil War". Texas Woman's University. https://twu.edu/media/documents/history-government/Propriety-Meets-Necessity-Female-Nuring-in-the-Civil-War.pdf.

Ward, Andrew. *River Run Red, The Fort Pillow Massacre in the Civil War*. Penguin, 2005.

Washington, Margaret. *Sojourner Truth's America*. University of Illinois Press, 2009.

"Women's Wartime Relief Associations". *Institute of Colored Youth in the Civil War Era Classes of 1856 to 1864*. https://exhibits.library.villanova.edu/institute-colored-youth/community-moments/icy-and-womens-wartime-relief-associations.

Wynn, Jake. "Mercy on the Mississippi: The USS Red Rover Hospital Ship". *National Museum of Civil War Medicine*. May 21, 2020. https://www.civilwarmed.org/redrover/.

"Yours for the Uplifting". *The Institute for Colored Youth in the Civil War Era Classes of 1856 to 1864*. https://exhibits.library.villanova.edu/institute-colored-youth/their-own-words/yours-uplifting-freedmens-schools-and-teacher-sarah-l-daffin.

Made in the USA
Coppell, TX
13 June 2024

33440947R00056